CIRIA REPORT 166   FEBRUARY 1997

CDM Regulations -
work sector guidance
for designers

prepared by

Ove Arup & Partners

CONSTRUCTION INDUSTRY RESEARCH AND INFORMATION ASSOCIATION
6 Storey's Gate, Westminster, London SW1P 3AU

Tel 0171-222 8891   Fax 0171-222 1708

e-mail: switchboard@ciria.org.uk
website: http://www.ciria.org.uk/ciria/

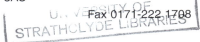

CDM Regulations - work sector guidance for designers
Construction Industry Research and Information Association
CIRIA Report 166, (1997)

Keywords

Construction (Design & Management) Regulations, construction work, demolition, design, designers, hazards, health and safety, maintenance, risk

Reader Interest

Construction industry designers, architects, civil engineers, structural engineers, services engineers, surveyors, consultants, local authorities, planning supervisors

CLASSIFICATION	
AVAILABILITY	Unrestricted
CONTENT	Guidance
STATUS	Committee guided
USER	on sector designers s, Architects, , Project Managers)

D
690.22
OVE

Executive Summary

This guidance provides assistance to designers for the identification of hazards in relation to the health and safety of construction workers and those affected by construction work. Through examples, some selected ways in which these hazards can be avoided, reduced or controlled are presented together with options designers may be able to employ in order to comply with the Construction (Design and Management) Regulations 1994, (CDM). Designers, through their imagination and technical ability, will doubtless think of many other ways and options which are more suited to the individual needs of their particular project. It is hoped that this document will promote this action.

Designers are intended to use this handbook as a first point of reference. They should then apply their own thinking to particular projects in order to identify the hazards so that, where it is reasonably practicable, these hazards are avoided or reduced. It is not the place of this report to identify all the hazards associated with a design and how they can be avoided or reduced. This is the designer's responsibility.

Section 1 of the report provides an introduction, explaining the limits of the guidance given. Section 2 contains the 38 individual work sectors and explains how the information is presented. Each of the work sectors has the same 4-page format, leading designers through the process of identifying hazards, then providing some options for amending the design to avoid the hazards, reduce the impact of hazards or introduce control measures of various types. The work sectors also indicate other elements of the project which may have a related impact and provides some references for further information on that particular topic.

Section 3 gives limited guidance on the legal requirements for designers to produce information as a direct result of the CDM Regulations. It also considers how the design process may be documented by designers for their own management purposes. This is not a requirement of the CDM Regulations, but may be held to be a sensible business practice.

General references for further guidance are given in Section 4 of this report and as the report is not intended to be entirely self supporting, it is recommended that users of the report have access to most of these references.

The scope of the 38 work sectors covered in this report limits the application of the guidance, however in selecting the topics to be addressed, the steering committee took as its aim the inclusion of those topics believed to result in the most common, numerous or significant risks to health and safety during construction and other work covered by the CDM Regulations.

This report contains references, etc, which are valid at February 1997. Legislation or guidance which appears after that date has not been taken into account.

CIRIA would welcome written feedback from users of this report, which should be addressed to David Churcher at CIRIA, as well as suggestions for additional work sectors which might be covered in future editions of the handbook.

Acknowledgements

The research work leading to this project was carried out by Ove Arup & Partners, under contract to CIRIA. The project supervisor was Allan Delves assisted by Paul Craddock, publication design was by Steven Groák. CIRIA's Research Manager for the project was David Churcher.

Work Sector Authors

The work sector authors were all drawn from the staff of Ove Arup & Partners

David Anderson	Howard Porter
Barry Austin	Gordon Puzey
Bob Cather	Mark Rudrum
Paul Craddock	Peter Ross
Allan Delves	Eric Wilde
Roger Drayton	Mel Wheeler
Roger Howkins	Library staff

Sketches and Graphics

The sketches were prepared by Fred English to whom a special vote of thanks is recorded. The graphics was undertaken by Denis Kirtley, Trevor Slydel and Martin Hall.

Project Steering Group

The research was guided by a Steering Group, established by CIRIA to advise on technical scope and presentation of content. This comprised:

Mr A D Rogerson (Chairman)	McDowells
Mr S Bell	Royal Institute of British Architects, CONIAC
Professor D Bishop	Construction Industry Council
Mr E Criswick	DoE Construction Sponsorship Directorate
Mr P Gray	Scott Wilson Kirkpatrick & Co Ltd
Mr H Hosker	Building Design Partnership
Mr D Lamont/Mr N Thorpe	Health and Safety Executive
Dr M Lockwood	Construction Industry Council
Mr B Mansell	Institution of Civil Engineers, CONIAC
Mr I Neil	Acer Consultants (latterly Hyder Consulting Ltd)
Mr R Oughton	F C Foreman & Partners
Mr J Read	WS Atkins Consultants Ltd
Mr P White/Mr T Hetherington	Health and Safety Executive
Mr D Williams	Balfour Beatty/Senior Safety Advisers Group

In addition, detailed technical comment on individual groups of work sectors was obtained from the following Review Groups, established by CIRIA:

Group A	Mr J Ahern	J Ahern & Associates
	Mr D Brattle	Lovell Construction
	Mr K Dew	John Pelling & Partners
	Mr E Kulikowski	John Laing Construction
	Mr B Mansell	Institution of Civil Engineers
	Mr P White	Health and Safety Executive

Group B	Mr S Corbet	G Maunsell & Partners
	Mr P Gray	Scott Wilson Kirkpatrick & Co Ltd
	Mr J Hatto	Bovis Construction Ltd
	Mr R Herring	Kier Engineering Services
	Mr B Norton, CBE	Federation of Civil Engineering Contractors
	Mr N Thorpe	Health and Safety Executive
Group C	Mr D Brown	Steel Construction Institute
	Mr D Chapman	Bovis Construction Ltd
	Mr K Dew	John Pelling & Partners
	Mr B Norton CBE	Federation of Civil Engineering Contractors
	Mr J Read	WS Atkins Consultants Ltd
	Mr M C Shurlock	Kier Engineering Services Ltd
	Mr B Todd	Kier Engineering Services Ltd
	Mr P White	Health and Safety Executive
	Mr P Williams	British Constructional Steelwork Association
Group D	Mr W Adams	Tilbury Douglas Construction
	Mr S Bell	RIBA, CONIAC
	Mr K Dew	John Pelling & Partners
	Mr J Elkington	NBS Services
	Mr H Hosker	Building Design Partnership
	Mr C Lawrence	Tilbury Douglas Construction
	Mr R Nanayakkara	BSRIA
	Mr R Oughton	F C Foreman & Partners
	Mr S Thompson	The Boyd Partnership, RIAU
	Mr N Thorpe	Health and Safety Executive
	Mr D Watson	WSP Group
Group E	Mr D Cowan	Laing Civil Engineering
	Mr J Modro	Balfour Beatty Civil Engineering
	Mr J Read	WS Atkins Consultants Ltd
	Dr L Smail	Union Railways (latterly Bechtel Ltd)
	Mr N Thorpe	Health and Safety Executive
	Mr P York	Highways Agency

The CI/SfB classification codes in each work sector were checked by Mr J Cann of NBS Services and Annette O'Brien of Ove Arup & Partners.

CIRIA and Ove Arup & Partners would like to express their thanks to all those individuals and organisations who took part in the consultation for this project, including the Steering Group and Review Groups.

Funding

The research project was funded by DoE Construction Sponsorship Directorate, the Health and Safety Executive, Institution of Civil Engineers Research & Development Enabling Fund, CIRIA's Core Programme, and from a contribution-in-kind from the research contractor.

Contents

1 Introduction

1.1 THE NEED FOR ACTION TO IMPROVE HEALTH AND SAFETY IN CONSTRUCTION

The chances of being killed during a working lifetime on construction sites are 1 in 300 and the chances of being disabled by serious illness or injury is much greater than for workers in other industries. In addition, members of the general public are also injured and killed by construction work. Provisional figures from the Health and Safety Executive indicate that 83 workers were killed on sites in 1995/96. An analysis of this figure into types of accident is given in Table 1.1. Although the total number of fatalities has decreased over recent years, the nature of accidents has remained broadly the same.

There is also a large incidence of health problems amongst construction workers and Table 1.2 gives estimates for numbers suffering ill-health as a result of certain hazards. These numbers dwarf the figures for injuries and on-the-job fatalities and in many cases, the effects may not be felt until years of exposure have taken place.

Table 1.1 *Breakdown of fatalities according to type of accident (Source: Health and Safety Executive)*

Percentage of total	Type of accident
56%	Falls from a height
21%	Trapped by something collapsing or overturning
10%	Struck by a moving vehicle
5%	Contact with electricity or an electrical discharge
4%	Struck by a falling/flying object during machine lifting of materials
3%	Contact with moving machinery or material being machined
1%	Exposure to a hot or harmful substance

Table 1.2 *Annual estimates of numbers suffering from work-related ill health in the construction industry (Source: Health and Safety Executive)*

Hazard (possible resulting disease or condition)	Estimated lower limit	Estimated upper limit
Asbestos (mesothelioma, asbestosis, lung cancer)	200-250 deaths	
Musculoskeletal injury (back disorders, work- related upper limb disorders, lower limb disorders, etc.)	30,000	48,000
Respiratory disease (bronchitis, emphysema, asthma, pneumoconiosis, sinusitis, influenza, etc.)	3,500	23,000
Skin disease	3,100	10,500
Noise (deafness and ear conditions)	1,000	5,800

From the figures in these tables, it is clear that great improvements can be made. To do so, contributions need to be made by clients, designers and contractors. In particular designers need access to guidance which will assist them in identifying the hazards arising from their design and then to avoid, reduce or control the hazards through the design process.

1.2　THE PURPOSE, SCOPE AND LIMITATIONS OF THIS GUIDANCE

This guidance has been produced to assist designers to comply with Regulation 13 (2) and 13 (3) of the Construction (Design & Management) Regulations 1994, (CDM). This Regulation requires designers to ensure that any design prepared for the purposes of 'construction work' during construction, maintenance, repair or demolition includes adequate regard to the avoidance and reduction of hazards, protection of all affected and protection of individual workers. The scope of a designer's responsibility under the CDM Regulations is outlined in the Approved Code of Practice, to which all designers should refer, together with the guidance by the Construction Industry Advisory Committee (CONIAC), *Designing for health and safety in construction* (Health and Safety Commission, 1994).

The purpose of this guidance is to help designers to meet their statutory duty in the following ways.

1.　It provides information on the major hazards associated with each of the specific work sectors.

2.　It gives key considerations, prompts and examples to encourage designers to think about the peculiarities of their own specific projects and to identify and prioritise project related hazards with respect to the stages of the design.

3.　Once the health and safety hazards have been identified, it provides signposts to the types of responses that designers can make to alter their design so as to avoid, reduce or control the hazards.

4.　It gives cross-references, both to other sectors of construction work addressed by the report which may be related in terms of health and safety, and to external texts from which further or more detailed information may be obtained.

The guidance has been drafted for designers who are active in design practice in any construction discipline and need rapid access to the key considerations connected with a particular construction work sector. Within each work sector, what can be achieved by the designer is influenced by the design stage and previous decisions that have been taken, either by the designer or by others.

The scope of this report is restricted to 38 work sectors, chosen following industry consultation and intended to represent those areas of construction work considered to contain the most significant and common hazards and risks to the health and safety of construction workers and others (e.g. members of the public and building occupiers). However, these work sectors by no means address all hazards in construction. Every designer has to think through the design options to identify all the hazards that can reasonably be foreseen and then act accordingly to avoid or reduce them.

A number of the hazards mentioned specifically in the work sectors, or those that designers may further identify, may be outside a particular designer's scope of control or may be issues that a principal contractor would deal with. However, they are included so that designers may be as fully informed as possible about the range of potential hazards. Those not familiar with site practices might find *Health and safety in construction*, HS(G)150 (Health and Safety Executive 1996), a useful introduction to the main health and safety hazards in construction work.

The designer's duties relate to considering hazards which can reasonably be identified and to provide information so that contractors and others can be made aware of them. Designers are not required to outline methods of dealing with hazards but should explain any particular construction assumptions that have been made as part of the design.

Readers need to appreciate that the guidance in this document is not intended to repeat information available elsewhere, but to include reference to it, so it is not intended that this handbook can be read entirely in isolation.

1.3 DEFINITIONS

1.3.1 'Designer' and 'construction work'

The CDM Regulations define the terms 'designer' and 'construction work' with much wider meanings than those in common construction usage. This report adheres to the definitions, which can be found in Regulation 2 (1).

The definition of 'design', which includes preparation of specifications and bills of quantities, widens the meaning of 'designer' to include surveyors, clients (when they specify particular requirements), project managers, specialist suppliers and contractors and temporary works designers. The consequence is that many more parties to a project will have duties under Regulation 13 than might otherwise be thought.

1.3.2 'Hazard' and 'risk'

The terms hazard and risk are defined in the CONIAC guidance *A guide to managing health and safety in construction* (Health and Safety Commission, 1995), as follows:

Hazard   Something with the potential to cause harm.
Risk   The likelihood that harm from a particular hazard will occur and the possible extent of the harm, i.e. severity.

These definitions have been adopted within this report.

1.3.3 Stages of a project

To provide continuity with previous publications, in particular, CIRIA Report 145 CDM *Regulations - case study guidance for designers: An interim report* (CIRIA 1995), the terms 'concept stage', 'scheme stage' and 'detail stage' have been used to subdivide the design process, remembering that much design is done after the appointment of the principal contractor.

The designer's response to any hazards identified will vary according to the stage of design development. There is more flexibility to avoid hazards at the start of the design process, during concept stage, than during the detail stage, when control measures may be more appropriate for dealing with any remaining hazards.

1.4 HOW TO USE THIS GUIDANCE

The work sectors have been arranged into five groups labelled A to E, each of which address a major area of construction work. Within each group the work sectors are referenced numerically. The arrangement of the groups has been organised to reflect the order of construction where possible.

Each of the 38 work sectors is referenced as **<Group letter><Work sector number>**.
For example:

'Deep basements and shafts' is referenced as **B2** (Group **B**, Work sector **2** in this group)

This referencing system is used for the internal cross-references between work sectors, principally in the sections headed Related Issues.

In some instances work sectors are intended to be read in conjunction with others, e.g. C1 (General concrete) should be read alongside any of the more specific concrete topics (C2, C3 or C4).

A detailed description of the way in which the work sectors are arranged is given in Section 2.

1.5 FLOWCHART OF HAZARD ANALYSIS

The guidance considers that designers can follow a logical process to deal with the hazards that have been identified, either as typical generic hazards or project specific. The outcome of this process will depend on the nature of the hazard and the limits of the project that is being considered. Figure 1.1 illustrates the process as a flowchart which starts with the identification of the hazards and concludes with the significant residual risks.

The three elements of Figure 1.1 are described below:

1. The design process is divided into three stages (concept, scheme and detail). Each design stage will address different issues, but typically the nature of issues will move from the general to the particular as the design is refined.

2. Once hazards have been identified, the CDM process is split into the three approaches (avoid, reduce, control), and each of these methods of solution to the problem is considered in turn. For example, reduction measures should be considered only if a hazard cannot reasonably be avoided.

3. The end of the hazard consideration in design process is the selection of the residual risks that remain in the design after steps 1 and 2, above, have been taken. Those which are judged to be significant or unusual in the context of the project need to be identified. Information on these risks will be provided to those who need it in order that appropriate action can be taken by the contractor, for construction, or the client for future work.

This process of analysing and dealing with hazards is considered in the work sectors under the headings of **Hazard Consideration in Design** and **Examples**. The Hazard Consideration in Design section within each work sector assumes a parallel series of operations to analyse the various risks arising from the intended construction. These then determine the degree of effort designers should apply to eliminating or reducing the hazards. This corresponds with the qualified nature of the designer's duties in the CDM Regulations which are **'so far as reasonably practicable'**.

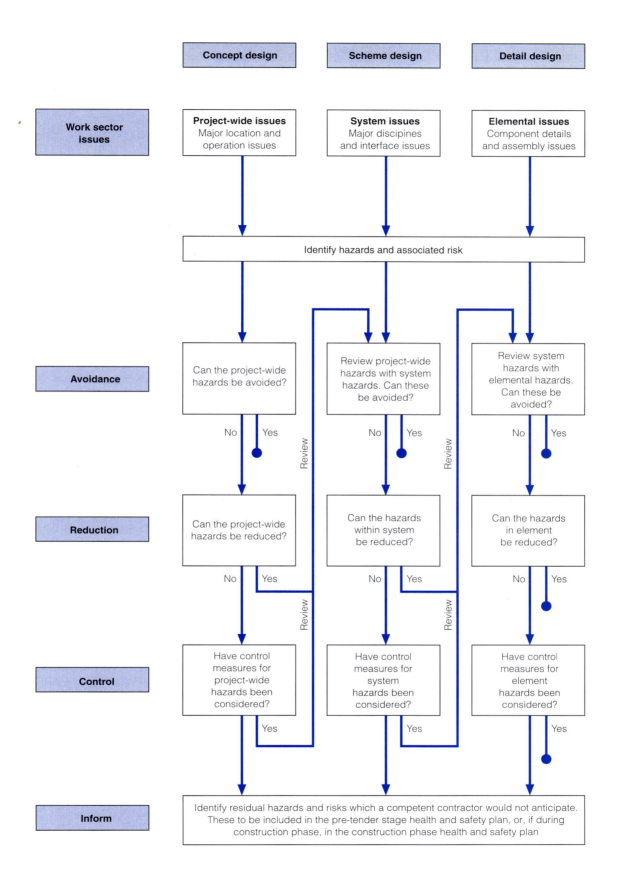

Figure 1.1 *Flowchart of hazard analysis*

1.6 PLANNING AND SEQUENCING OF CONSTRUCTION

At concept stage, the designers of a project can do a great deal to avoid and reduce significant hazards. One technique to be used to achieve this is to alter the way the construction is planned including the sequence of construction that is assumed. This is a powerful tool, but it requires wide understanding of the construction process and of the options that are feasible.

Examples:

1 Designers can reduce the potential for health problems arising from manual handling by producing a scheme that encourages mechanical lifting during maintenance operations and places a limit on the weight of objects to be handled manually.

2 Designers can reduce the need to work at height when erecting a steel frame by designing the steelwork in modular sections which can be pre-fabricated at ground level and sequentially lifted into place. This does not eliminate working at height entirely but should reduce it significantly. The safety of those who do have to work at height can further be enhanced if the ground slab is installed before the steel frame so as to provide a stable, flat working surface from which mobile elevating work platforms can be used for bolting up. This is much safer than using ladder access and quicker than scaffolding.

1.6.1 Assess alternative plans/sequences of construction

Although designers are not expected to specify particular construction methods or sequences, they will be expected to have considered possible alternatives when the hazards are being identified. If the assumptions of construction method and sequence become inextricably woven into the design, such that there is only one reasonable choice, then this will have to be made known.

Alternative methods and sequences will need to be considered to ensure that the appropriate choice is made. This will include factors other than health and safety and the final choice will reflect that health and safety is not expected to be pursued at any cost, rather that decisions have to be sensible and reasonable and balanced with other design decisions.

Table 1.3 *Example assessment of alternative methods and sequences of construction*

Consideration	Option 1: Assemble in-situ	Option 2: Pre-assemble and lift into place
Health and safety	Operatives working at height, risk of people falling, risk of falling objects, risk of lifting many individual items	Fewer operatives working at height, risks from manipulating large modules, quicker site operation means shorter exposure times.
Quality	Variable quality	Better opportunities for quality control
Programme	Assembly in-situ slower than prefabricating	Quicker than assembling in-situ in terms of site work. Pre-assembly can be elsewhere on site or remote. Requires longer lead time.
Price	Usually little difference in cost of materials and components. Pre-assembly possibly more expensive in total manpower/double handling, needs larger crane, etc.	
Performance	In this instance, it is judged that there is no material difference in eventual performance of the structure arising from the choice of one construction method or another.	

2   Work sector guidance

2.1   WORK SECTOR GROUPS

The work sectors in this report are divided into five groups, relating to main stages of construction work, as follows:

Group A	General planning
Group B	Excavation and foundations
Group C	Primary structure
Group D	Building elements and building services
Group E	Civil engineering

Within these groups, each of the 38 work sectors is presented in a standard format over four pages. Once readers are familiar with the layout and arrangement of the guidance material, it is expected that individual work sectors will be referred to on a case-by-case basis and the structure of the guidance has been designed with this in mind. However, it is vital that users of the material have read and understood the Introduction to the report and also have access to the list of general reference material contained in Section 4 of the report.

2.2   THE CONTENT OF EACH PART OF THE WORK SECTOR STRUCTURE

Each of the work sectors is arranged over four pages, with a common structure of headings and subdivision of the information presented.

The following notes indicate what each part of the common structure of the work sector guidance contains. In order to get maximum benefit from the guidance, readers must know where within each work sector particular information is contained.

Table 2.1 *Description of contents of each work sector*

Page reference	Heading used	Contents
Page 1	Scope	This describes what the work sector covers, either as a formal definition or as examples in bullet point form.
	Exclusions	This describes what is not included in the scope of the work sector, usually items which have been considered too specialist.
	Major Hazards	These are hazards that will be most likely to arise when this work sector is included in a construction project. (A maximum of 6 are given, to concentrate on the major issues.)
Page 2	Specific Hazard Identification	This section gives typical issues that may arise, depending on the nature of the project the designer is undertaking, to add to those identified in "Major Hazards". There are examples of specific questions, headed "Possible key considerations". These are included to stimulate lateral thought, as it is obviously impossible for any guidance of this kind to cover all possible eventualities. This list works in conjunction with the "Prompts".
	Prompts	This gives a list of general issues which may well influence how the key considerations are addressed. The list is NOT exhaustive and each Prompt should be tested against each consideration.
	Hazard Consideration in Design	This section considers the issues that might arise at different stages of the design process (concept, scheme and detail), ranging from strategic questions at concept stage to specific issues at later stages. This section also presents some possible design options which could allow the designer to avoid or reduce health and safety hazards. The design options are a starting point and must not be considered as a complete list.
Page 3	Examples of Risk Mitigation (methods of solution)	This sub-section considers typical issues showing how these generate different responses, according to whether the hazard can be avoided or only reduced, or whether control measures are required as a last resort.
	Examples of Risk Mitigation (issues addressed at different stages)	This sub-section presents two typical projects to illustrate how a particular issue can be addressed in different ways as the design progresses from concept to detail stage.
Page 4	Related Issues	This section identifies other work sectors within the report which have an impact on, or are affected by, the work sector in question. Work sectors are referenced by their letter number - see section 1.4.
	References for Further Guidance	This gives titles of other published guidance, arranged as primary, secondary and background references. General references which apply to the report as a whole are given in Section 4 of the report. The classification of this work sector in the Common Arrangement of Work Sectors, Civil Engineering Work Sectors and CI/SfB systems is also given where appropriate.

Group A - General planning
1 - Surrounding environment

Read the Introduction (page 9) before using the following guidelines

Scope

- Infrastructure - roads, railways, waterways, airport - load, length, width, height requirements.
- Adjacent environment - residential, commercial, industrial, conservation, leisure, civil.
- Transportation - plant, materials, personnel, to/from site, emergency facilities
- Occupation and activities of existing environment.
- Working procedures in an occupied building, etc.
- Topography - mining, lakes, rivers, quarries, caves, reservoirs, tidal areas.
- Adjacent structures and services - tall, basements, foundations, pipes, overhead cables, road, rail.
- Air rights (oversailing), railway rights, navigation rights.
- Site access, availability - parking, storage, road closures, low bridges, special access for surveys to railways, rivers, etc.

Exclusions

- Special types of neighbourhood (e.g. nuclear installations, defence establishments).

Major Hazards

Refer to the Introduction (page 9) for details of accident types and health risks

Falls
Work area perimeter security, preventing unauthorised access to active work areas.

Plant movement
Onto and off site plant and transportation loads/access/routes/noise.

Collapse
Working adjacent to previous excavations or existing/adjacent structures, old mine workings.

Services
Existing services, overhead, underground, buried, unknown, on-site, in buildings.

Impact
Plant lifting/over-sailing above local sensitive areas, shopping areas, schools, pavements, roads.

Health hazards
Dust, emissions from adjacent premises, dumps, sewers, ground seepage.
Contaminated land.

GENERAL PLANNING **A 1**

EXCAVATIONS AND FOUNDATIONS **B**

PRIMARY STRUCTURE **C**

BUILDING ELEMENTS AND BUILDING SERVICES **D**

CIVIL ENGINEERING **E**

A1 GENERAL PLANNING

B EXCAVATIONS AND FOUNDATIONS

C PRIMARY STRUCTURE

D BUILDING ELEMENTS AND BUILDING SERVICES

E CIVIL ENGINEERING

Specific Hazard Identification

Possible key considerations:

- **Surroundings** - What are the health hazards in the proximity (airborne, buried, industrial, commercial liquid/dust/solid, etc.)?
- **Infrastructure** - Where is the review of the infrastructure to ensure that it is able safely to support site traffic (load, frequency, duration, etc.)?
- **Project** - What health hazards will the project construction place on the surrounding environment?
- **Methods** - Where have those situations that require method statements or controls been identified?
- **Information** - How will information be obtained from the client?
- **Services** - What hazards exist from surroundings (buried services, overhead cables, etc.)?
- **Any others?**

Prompts

- Road infrastructure
- Rail/air/water transportation
- Services in site proximity
- Sequence of construction
- Ground conditions
- Sensitive areas/noise, vibration
- Offsite deposit
- Offsite storage
- Fire
- Emergency services

Hazards Consideration in Design

Stage	Considerations and issues	Possible design options to avoid or mitigate hazards identified from surrounding environment
Concept Design	• Why build here? • Infrastructure scope • Neighbours assessed? • Shift working • Local climate • Access routes for site	• Reduce contaminated ground hazards by containment. • Avoid open excavation to reduce hazards of adjacent contaminated ground. • Consider if the area poses increased risks of fire, flood or other hazards to site. • Ensure that local roads and infrastructure can carry the elements (as designed) without hazard to operatives/public.
Scheme Design	• Known contamination • Adjacent structures • Adjacent emissions • Oversailing adjacent buildings/areas • Pollutants • Local transport • Topography • Sensitive areas	• Design to suit local conditions, e.g. avoid basements in flooded ground; avoid work at height in exposed areas. • Use shafts and headings to avoid need for deep open trenches. • Foundations to suit site ground conditions (e.g. sheet piling in loose ground). • Avoid over-sailing adjacent property, fix windows from within building.
Detail Design	• External services • Existing structures • Security of site working • Vehicle movements • Sequence restrictions • Time restrictions	• If shift or extended sequence of work required, design for off-site fabrication, minimise site activities. • For work in restricted areas, adapt the design (e.g. avoid brickwork in tidal excavations, use pre-cast elements - plastic or cast iron pipework). • Design to avoid existing services rather than re-route them.

Group A - General planning
1 - Surrounding environment

Examples of Risk Mitigation (methods of solution)

Examples of Risk Mitigation (issues addressed at different stages)

Old properties adjacent to the site are founded upon made-up ground. The basement of the new building is to cover part of the site and extends up to the adjacent party walls. The facade of the building on the site is to be retained, but is presently founded at a higher level than the proposed new building foundations.

Concept design	Scheme design	Detail design
To reduce the risk of collapse of adjacent structures resulting from ground movement, the designer has redesigned the new basement.	Allow the new structure to provide support to the facade during construction, avoiding temporary supports.	The designer will outline the procedures for supporting the retained facade during construction.

A new sewage treatment plant for a small town has been relocated, at feasibility study stage, due to surrounding ground conditions. However, the new location will require a longer route for the main sewer. The new sewer pipe has to pass through areas of existing services and has to withstand a high water table.

Concept design	Scheme design	Detail design
Designers are seeking ways of reducing costs of the increased length of main sewer, mindful of health and safety.	A design review identifies opportunities to reduce hazards of trench excavation through zones of existing services, by review of detailed alignment.	Access chambers will be designed in pre-cast concrete to include details that will reduce site activities in continuously pumped excavations.

Related Issues

References within this document

References	Related issues
A2	Site clearance activities will need to consider environment.
A3	Site investigation may confirm significant surrounding influences.
A4	Access onto the site is likely to be determined by surrounding environment.
A5	Site layout will be affected by the surroundings and access requirements.
B1-B3	Excavation planning needs to consider surroundings, underground, overhead services, etc.
B5-B7	Foundations may undermine or load surroundings.
C1-C4	Concrete materials brought to site in bulk.
C5-C6	Structural steel may require special access to site.
C7	Timber may be influenced by the surrounding environment.
C8	Masonry materials will require regular access to site for deliveries.
D5	Surface coatings/finishes may require special protection to prevent unsafe spreading during application.
D1	External cladding will need access and off-loading facilities.
D6	Cleaning buildings may oversail adjacent properties.
D7-D9	Services will be influenced by demands from site.
E2	Roads may affect access/egress limits to the site.
E3	Railways may assist or constrain the site access.

References for Further Guidance

Primary general references and background information given in Section 4

Primary

- CIRIA Report 64 Noise from Construction and Demolition Sites 1977(microfiche)
- CIRIA Special Publication 96 Environmental assessment - A guide to the identification, evaluation and mitigation of environmental issues in construction schemes 1994
- HSE HS (G)66 Protection of workers and the general public during the development of contaminated land
- BRE GS DD175 Fire and explosion hazards associated with the redevelopment of contaminated land Information paper 2, 1987

Secondary

- DoT Safety at Streetworks and Roadworks: A Code of Practice 1993

Background

- CIRIA Special Publications 93 & 94 Environmental issues in construction - A review of issues and initiatives relevant to the building, construction and related industries (volumes 1 and 2) 1993
- CIRIA Special Publication 97 Environmental handbook - Design and specification 1994
- CIRIA Special Publication 98 Environmental handbook - Construction phase 1994
- CIRIA Special Publication 111 Remedial treatment of contaminated land Vol XI: Planning and management 1995
- BS DD175:1988(1992) Draft code of practice for the identification of potentially contaminated land and its investigation

Classification

CAWS Group A,   **CEWS** Class A,   **CI/SfB** Code (--)(H)

Group A - General planning
2 - Site clearance (and small scale demolition)

A2

Read the Introduction (page 9) before using the following guidelines

Scope

- Earth moving - loading, transporting, placing.
- Tree-felling, mast/pole/post.
- Waste removal - safe, toxic, suitable transport, licensed tip.
- Excavation - clays, granular, rock material, contaminated ground.
- Water removal - fresh, salt, foul, brackish, contamination of water courses.
- Services - above/below ground, tunnels, pipes, wires, diversions, relocations.
- Structures - above/below ground, party walls.
- Demolition - brickwork, timber, concrete, steel, asbestos, lead-based paints, etc.
- Partial removal of clearance/demolition.

Exclusions

- Special conditions - unusual, unstable, (e.g. shallow mine workings).
- Radio-active areas.
- Below water - use of divers, dredging, etc.
- Buried explosives - mines, terrorist action.

Major Hazards

Refer to the Introduction (page 9) for details of accident types and health risks

Collapse of excavation
Buried obstructions, underground voids, unexpectedly poor ground conditions, water table.

Health hazards
Toxic waste, decomposing materials causing gaseous emissions, asbestos, microbiological agents.

Flooding/Fire/Explosion
From underground or above ground services.

Services/electrocution
Underground services, overhead cables, fixed equipment on site.

Falling from height
Loose/unstable material, access, inadequate support.

Noise/vibration/dust
Breaking-up of building fabric with mechanical breakers, asbestos, silica.

GENERAL PLANNING — A2
EXCAVATIONS AND FOUNDATIONS — B
PRIMARY STRUCTURE — C
BUILDING ELEMENTS AND BUILDING SERVICES — D
CIVIL ENGINEERING — E

A
2
GENERAL PLANNING

B
EXCAVATIONS AND FOUNDATIONS

C
PRIMARY STRUCTURE

D
BUILDING ELEMENTS AND BUILDING SERVICES

E
CIVIL ENGINEERING

Specific Hazard Identification

Possible key considerations:

- **Previous uses** - Where have previous uses of site been established?
- **Site survey** - When was a full site survey carried out?
- **Hazardous materials** - What are procedures to deal with hazardous materials?
- **Toxicity** - What is extent of hazardous materials' volume/toxicity, particularly asbestos?
- **Clearance** - Clearance causes dust hazards: prepare plans to define and contain it.
- **Unstable site** - Is the site unstable? Will clearance cause instability? Review any risks of flooding.
- **Demolition** - How are structures constructed and will it affect methods of demolition?
- **Handling** - What materials during clearance are hazardous to handle?
- **Services** - Identify existing above/below ground services and installations.
- **Any others?**

Prompts

- Existing health and safety file
- Client information
- Site records/drawings
- Investigation results
- Fill source
- Site security
- Site access
- Sequence of working
- Structural records
- Plant routes
- Personnel routes
- Health
- Fire

Hazards Consideration in Design

Stage	Considerations and issues	Possible design options to avoid or mitigate hazards identified for site clearance
Concept Design	• Location - why here? • Bulk transport capability • Hazardous materials • Previous site use • Flood prevention	• Ensure complete up-to-date description of existing site services. • Build remote from major existing services. • Avoid trees, rather than remove and replace.
Scheme Design	• Demolition • Phasing activities • Transport plan • Site contamination • Surveys/records known • Clearance methods • Demolition method • Elemental clearance • Sequencing of work • Stability of ground • Stability of structures	• Seal contaminated ground on site, if possible, rather than excavate and replace with fill. • Store and re-use material on site; avoid transportation off-site. • Avoid existing services rather than protect them. • Design service diversions to avoid/minimise site clearance. • Design new foundation to avoid existing obstructions.
Detail Design	• Clearance activities • Demolition procedure • Landscape profile	• Optimise site filling with excavated material (cut and fill). • Use site demolition material as hard-core fill. • Use driven piled foundations through contaminated ground, to minimise open excavation.

Group A - General planning
2 - Site clearance (and small scale demolition)

A2

GENERAL PLANNING **A 2**

EXCAVATIONS AND FOUNDATIONS **B**

PRIMARY STRUCTURE **C**

BUILDING ELEMENTS AND BUILDING SERVICES **D**

CIVIL ENGINEERING **E**

Examples of Risk Mitigation (methods of solution)

ACTION / ISSUE	Contaminated ground	Demolition of large house on new development
Avoidance Design to avoid identified hazards but beware of introducing others	Proposed structures relocated, ground not disturbed.	Incorporate house into overall scheme with possible conversion to flats.
Reduction Design to reduce identified hazards but beware of increasing others	Contaminated ground identified and sealed.	Highlight site constraints.
Control Design to provide acceptable safeguards for all remaining identified hazards	Contaminated ground removed under controlled monitoring.	Recommend a sequence of demolition following survey.

Examples of Risk Mitigation (issues addressed at different stages)

A small enabling works contract is to be let for site clearance prior to the main contract. The site is adjacent to a main road which is particularly busy during rush hours. There are also colleges and schools in the area, so the pavements are usually crowded. The site clearance requires some ground works excavation and hardstanding. The site is to be fenced and made secure.

Concept design	Scheme design	Detail design
Careful consideration will be given to site layout and the surrounding environment, in order to reduce number of traffic movements.	Location of the site entrance and access roads will be planned to reduce hazards of site transport activities accessing and leaving the site.	The site entrance is designed to allow measures to be implemented to control site traffic across the pavement access.

Several properties dating from the late 19th century are to be demolished to allow for a new development. There are no construction drawings for the largest building on the site and the method of construction for this building will require to be established before demolition planning can take place. The building has been modified on several occasions since it was originally built.

Concept design	Scheme design	Detail design
The existing building will be surveyed in order to identify the structural systems and key demolition issues.	Part of the building is load-bearing brickwork with pre-stressed concrete slabs and beams. Information to be included in the pre-tender stage H&S Plan, to alert tendering contractors to demolition hazards.	To control site hazards of sudden failure, pre-stressed beams and slabs to be removed and broken up in a controlled condition at ground level. This is considered less hazardous than propping all the elements and breaking them up at height.

Related Issues

References within this document

References	Related issues
A4	Access onto/within the site to be kept clear and safe during site clearance.
A5	Site layout plays an important part in site clearance and following activities.
A1	Surrounding environment will need to be protected from the hazards of site clearance and demolition.
A3	Site investigation will be early and may need to interface with site clearance.
B1	General excavation could be part of or follow site clearance.
B2	Deep basement excavation could be required to interface with site clearance.
B3	Trenches for foundations/services for early enabling works.
B4	Retaining wall excavation may interface with site clearance.
B5	Ground stabilization may be needed before or after site clearance activities.
B6	Piling foundations will interface with site clearance and may form part of it.
B7	Foundation underpinning before or after site clearance.
E1	Small civil engineering works likely before or after site clearance .
E2	Work adjacent to roads needs to be considered together with all other public areas.
E3	Work adjacent to railways will have procedural implications on clearance and demolition.

References for Further Guidance

Primary general references and background information given in Section 4

Primary

- HSE HS(G) 66 Protection of workers and the general public during the redevelopment of contaminated land
- HSE GS5 Entry into confined spaces
- HSE GS29 Parts 1 to 4 Health and safety in demolition work
- CIRIA Special Publication 78 Building on derelict land 1991
- DoT, Interdepartmental Committee on the Redevelopment of Contaminated Land (ICRCL) Guidance Note 17/78 Notes on the development and after-use of landfill sites 1990

Secondary

- CIRIA Special Publication 38 Simple noise screens for site use 1985
- CIRIA Report 97 Trenching practice 1992

Background

- BS 6031:1981 Code of Practice for Earthworks
- Institute of Demolition Engineers Orchard W.R Elements of Risk and Safety Management in Demolition and Dismantling Projects
- Institute of Demolition Engineers Seminar Proceedings Demolition and the CDM Regulations, 1994

Classification

CAWS Group A&C, **CEWS** Class D,E,I,J,K,L,R,T,X&Y, **CI/SfB** Code (1-)(D2)

Read the Introduction (page 9) before using the following guidelines

Scope

- Structural surveys - including those in confined spaces.
- Building services surveys.
- Materials survey (e.g. asbestos, lead-based paint).
- Ground/soil sampling.
- Topographical/ground movement surveys.
- Rock coring.
- Boreholes/deep drilling at small diameter.
- Trial pits and excavations.
- Field testing - in-situ tests.
- Existing services location/inspection - pipes, cables, sewers.

Exclusions

- Testing - e.g. underwater.
- Traffic surveys.
- Use of specialist equipment - towers, scaffolds, jetties etc.

Major Hazards

Refer to the Introduction (page 9) for details of accident types and health risks

Inadequate working space
Width, height for identified situations, entrapment, awkward heavy lifting, manoeuvring.

Inadequate working platform
Capacity to support load/weight, slope instability, underground voids.

Working environment
Ventilation, illumination, hearing, tripping, collision, falling through openings or from edges.

Excavation collapse
Depth/dimensions for soil conditions, water table shoring, supervision, descent, falling, collapse, slip.

Health hazards
Noxious fumes, toxic, corrosive, explosive, microbiological, burial grounds.

Services
Excavation, drilling.
Sampling/testing.
Location of existing services.

A3 GENERAL PLANNING

B EXCAVATIONS AND FOUNDATIONS

C PRIMARY STRUCTURE

D BUILDING ELEMENTS AND BUILDING SERVICES

E CIVIL ENGINEERING

Specific Hazard Identification

Possible key considerations:

- **Route** - Where are adequate provisions for access to investigation point?
- **Access** - Plan adequate room for access around investigation zone?
- **Stability** - Have you ensured that the site or working platform is stable?
- **Contamination** - How is the contamination to be treated?
- **Services** - Where have services been located/exposed/disconnected?
- **Environment** - How will environmental control in confined spaces be done?
- **Equipment** - Where have you identified heavy equipment to be used?
- **Existing structures** - What effect will investigation have on existing structures and/or existing services?
- **What is the age and condition of buildings?**
- **Any others?**

Prompts

- Access routes
- Services
- Desk study
- Sequence of investigation
- Work access
- Site hoardings
- Health
- Fire
- Method statements

Hazards Consideration in Design

Stage	Considerations and issues	Possible design options to avoid or mitigate hazards identified for site investigation
Concept Design		• Check that sources of existing information will be able to provide relevant information. • Consider the likely completeness and accuracy of available information and the practicality of obtaining an independent survey or investigation.
Scheme Design	• Location - why here? • Previous use/surveys • Existing features • Access/exposure • Unknown features • Scope of survey • Stability of site • Working environment • Hazardous materials • Existing conditions • Survey equipment • Contamination • Setting out probes • Investigation access • Existing services • Temporary works • Specific conditions	• If weather has an influence on the intended investigation, check or define the preferred period of execution. • Review whether the investigation team could be better informed or protected by a pre-investigation survey or cleansing operation.
Detail Design		• Relate the distribution of boreholes, etc to the location and size of potential voids/obstructions but with respect to accessibility and potential buried obstructions. • Highlight risks with the use of electricity in particular situations.

Examples of Risk Mitigation (methods of solution)

ACTION \ ISSUE	Structural behaviour	Site exploration
Avoidance Design to avoid identified hazards but beware of introducing others	Previous structural drawings exist.	Boreholes samples and laboratory testing.
Reduction Design to reduce identified hazards but beware of increasing others	Pre-demolition structural survey.	Trial pits sampling.
Control Design to provide acceptable safeguards for all remaining identified hazards	Ensure technical demolition supervision.	In- situ field tests.

Examples of Risk Mitigation (issues addressed at different stages)

A soils site investigation is to be carried out. It is known that various live services cross the site. Measures will be required to be taken to avoid damaging live services and causing injury to operatives carrying out the site investigation.

Concept design	Scheme design	Detail design
Soils investigation, where possible, will be set out to avoid areas of known live services.	Exploration points are required in areas of existing services. To reduce the hazard, starter pits will be used for boreholes in close proximity to live services.	To reduce the hazard of live services, arrange for isolation of existing services not required, prior to starting site investigation work.

A group of buildings are to be extensively refurbished. Some drawings of the existing buildings are missing and existing services drawings are particularly incomplete. The services will be substantially replaced with a fully air-conditioned building.

Concept design	Scheme design	Detail design
A site investigation will be carried out to set-out existing services and insulation, to identify hazards from services and possible asbestos insulation.	During the survey to locate existing services, extensive asbestos insulation was found. The concept design was amended to avoid this hazard.	Designer sets down control procedures for isolating existing services and removing hazardous insulation prior to refurbishment activities.

GENERAL PLANNING — A3

EXCAVATIONS AND FOUNDATIONS — B

PRIMARY STRUCTURE — C

BUILDING ELEMENTS AND BUILDING SERVICES — D

CIVIL ENGINEERING — E

A
3
GENERAL PLANNING

B
EXCAVATIONS AND FOUNDATIONS

C
PRIMARY STRUCTURE

D
BUILDING ELEMENTS AND BUILDING SERVICES

E
CIVIL ENGINEERING

Related Issues

References within this document

References	Related issues
A2	Ground contamination will influence precautions required for spoil disposal
A2	Demolition strategy to be incorporated into brief for site investigation.
A4	Work in areas liable to flooding will generate special access requirements.
A4	Work on slopes may create stability problems and will generate special access requirements.
A5	Layout and structural capacity of existing buildings may influence feasibility and location of internal borings.
B1	Reinstatement of boreholes and pits to be considered in the design of any future excavation or foundation work.
B5	Shoring of trial pits will depend on stability of ground as assessed in the field.

References for Further Guidance

Primary general references and background information given in Section 4

Primary

- The Electricity Association, Avoidance of danger from underground electricity cables
- British Gas, Precautions to be taken when working in the vicinity of underground gas pipes
- HSE HS(G)47 Avoiding danger from underground services
- HSE GS5 Entry into confined spaces
- HSE HS(G)66 Protection of workers and the general public during the development of contaminated land
- CIRIA Special Publication 25 Site investigation manual 1983
- CIRIA Special Publication 73 Roles and responsibility in site investigation 1991
- CIRIA Special Publication 102-111 Remedial treatment for contaminated land - Vol 2-11 1995/96

Secondary

- CIRIA Report 97 Trenching practice 1992
- HSE GS6 Avoidance of danger from overhead electric lines

Background

- BS5930: 1981 Code of Practice for Site Investigation

Classification

CAWS Group D, **CEWS** Class B, **CI/SfB** Code (1-)(A3s)

Read the Introduction (page 9) before using the following guidelines

Scope

- Site perimeter - appropriate site access and security, boundary constraints.
- Site perimeter/building relationship - storage, handling and layout areas, welfare areas.
- Protection, illumination, visibility, ventilation, escape routes designed in.
- Building/structure, envelope, sequence of building operations.
- Emergency routes, compartmentation during construction, escape routes protection.
- Width, height, length, curvature, load - carrying capacity, overhead cables/services.
- Movement of personnel, vehicles, plant, materials.
- Site horizontal movement - roads, railways, waterways, footways, conveyors.
- Site vertical movement - stairs, ramps, shutes, hoists, cranes, pumps, cradles, lifts.

Exclusions

- Specialist access - aerial lifts, helicopters, abseiling, etc.
- Unstable structures - bomb-blasted, fire-damaged, defective, partial failure, etc.
- Tunnels and shafts.
- Radio-active contaminated areas.

Major Hazards

Refer to the Introduction (page 9) for details of accident types and health risks

Inadequate access
Width, height for identified situations. Capacity to withstand load/weight. Overhead cables.

Access to height/depth
Height, falling, struck. Depth; entrapment, asphyxiation, drowning.

Manoeuvring vehicles, plant and materials
Turning reversing, clearance, height, width. Two-way traffic, lack of storage layout.

Lifting, lowering loads
Clearance, lifting, slewing, handling, visibility, site lines, capacity, oversailing public access areas.

Working environment
Noise, non-separation of plant and people, poor visibility.

Polluted, contaminated access
Poor ventilation, poor illumination, dust, damp, dirt.

GENERAL PLANNING **A 4**

EXCAVATIONS AND FOUNDATIONS **B**

PRIMARY STRUCTURE **C**

BUILDING ELEMENTS AND BUILDING SERVICES **D**

CIVIL ENGINEERING **E**

Group A - General planning
4 - Access (onto and within site)

A
4
GENERAL PLANNING

B
EXCAVATIONS
AND FOUNDATIONS

C
PRIMARY STRUCTURE

D
BUILDING ELEMENTS
AND BUILDING SERVICES

E
CIVIL ENGINEERING

Specific Hazard Identification

Possible key considerations:

- **Access** - Plan adequate provision for access at site perimeter?
- **Site traffic** - Where will site traffic cross a public road, pavement and/or existing services to gain access to the site?
- **Access zone** - Ensure there is adequate room for access around/over the construction zone within the site at all levels.
- **Sequence** - Where will access within the site have to change as construction progresses?
- **Constraints** - Does the client's on-going business affect the work area, e.g. supermarket, hotel, process plant?
- **Separation** - Set out separation of vehicles/plant and from operatives activities.
- **Interfaces** - Carefully identify vehicles/plant/operatives crossings/interfaces.
- **Lifting zone** - Where have you identified lifting zones (locate cranes/hoists)?
- **Site layout** - Where have you identified delivery, laydown and storage areas to reduce manual handling and allow for mechanical lifting appliances?
- **Any others?**

Prompts

- Public - pedestrian, vehicular
- Plant and machinery routes
- Pedestrian routes
- Manual handling
- Mechanical lifting
- Movement of large units
- Existing services - divert?
- Overhead cables - divert?
- Lifting zones
- Restrictions, weight, size
- Emergency services
- Access routes
- Materials routes
- Storage areas
- Work areas
- Welfare areas
- Health issues
- Sequence of construction
- Fire
- Security

Hazards Consideration in Design

Stage	Considerations and issues	Possible design options to avoid or mitigate hazards identified for access (onto and within site)
Concept Design		• Traffic study to improve layout of site entrance and access. • Ensure phased completion maintains construction access routes. • Identify adequate site access to allow the design to be built safely. • Design to maintain emergency access to site.
Scheme Design	• Location - why here? • Main access, egress • Building activities • Emergency services • Site perimeter secure • Footprint of structure/building • Access within site and around building systems • Within perimeter • Movements in space between elements	• Design of permanent works to allow adequate temporary site access. • Design to provide for safe access to repair and maintain the building. • If access is conditional upon sequence, define the necessary sequence for safety throughout. • Emergency - identify and display services isolation points.
Detail Design	• Access in relation to site elements • Access to each building element	• Consider the likely working space required for safe construction of the various elements. • Consider the site work location (e.g. avoid site welding over/near public). • Consider light, ventilation and time available for the site activity. • In emergencies, workforce accessible to paramedics and stretchers.

Examples of Risk Mitigation (methods of solution)

ACTION \ ISSUE	Deliveries to city site building	Framed building construction
Avoidance — Design to avoid identified hazards but beware of introducing others	Design to allow lorries to unload within building footprint.	Design for permanent stairways to be installed as part of frame.
Reduction — Design to reduce identified hazards but beware of increasing others	Design components to be packaged to reduce unloading time in road.	Design fixings inside lift shafts to support temporary stairs.
Control — Design to provide acceptable safeguards for all remaining identified hazards	Highlight need to plan deliveries at off peak periods.	Highlight hazards involved when using ladders.

Examples of Risk Mitigation (issues addressed at different stages)

A city development site has very restricted access. The design team have agreed that special consideration will have to be given throughout the design to the particular difficulties of accessing this project during construction and subsequent maintenance.

Concept design	Scheme design	Detail design
To avoid site access difficulties, elements to have overall envelope of not more than 10m length x 3m x 2m x 20 tonnes.	To reduce site access hazards of the large atrium roof spans, a review of the structural element option has identified steel roof trusses as the preferred option.	Detail design hazards will be avoided with a steel roof truss to be designed for final assembly at ground level on site and then lifted into position.

A hospital has been planned to have the plant room for major plant at basement level.

Concept design	Scheme design	Detail design
Provision will be made for 4 boilers in the plantroom at basement level. Only 3 boilers will be installed during construction, through temporary works access over the plantroom.	The design will allow for a dedicated access route for boiler maintenance, removal and installation of the 4th boiler.	Design load and space checks on dedicated plant access route to include boilers, trolleys, lifting beams and winch points.

GENERAL PLANNING — A 4

EXCAVATIONS AND FOUNDATIONS — B

PRIMARY STRUCTURE — C

BUILDING ELEMENTS AND BUILDING SERVICES — D

CIVIL ENGINEERING — E

A 4 GENERAL PLANNING

B EXCAVATIONS AND FOUNDATIONS

C PRIMARY STRUCTURE

D BUILDING ELEMENTS AND BUILDING SERVICES

E CIVIL ENGINEERING

Related Issues

References within this document

References	Related issues
A1	Surrounding environment will have an influence on the way that the site is accessed.
A2	Site clearance strategy to be incorporated into early phases of access planning of the site.
A5	Site layout of temporary and permanent works will have a considerable influence on the access plan, ensure sealing (fire protection) during construction.
B1-B4	Excavation may affect the phasing of access to the various work faces as well as the site perimeter.
B6	Piling planning should maintain adequate access to the site.
C5,C6	Structural steel erection will affect both horizontal and vertical movement, limiting access for other activities.
D1	Cladding delivery, storage, lifting, positioning and fixing require detailed consideration of access routes.
D4	Windows/glazing, because they are fragile require careful integration into the works sequence, perhaps with temporary dedicated access.
E2	Permanent road construction will need to be considered when sequencing the temporary/permanent site access plan.
E4,E5	Bridge construction/maintenance is likely to require specialised access to carry out the work.
E6	Work over water will generate access requirements that are equally, if not more, demanding than land-based work.

References for Further Guidance

Primary general references and background information given in Section 4

Primary

- CIRIA Special Publication 121 Temporary access to the workface 1995
- HSE (G)47 Avoiding danger from underground services
- HSE GS5 Entry into confined spaces
- HSE GS6 Avoidance of danger from overhead electric lines

Secondary

- CIRIA Special Publication 131 Stability of cranes on site 1996
- HSE CIS5 (revised) Temporarily suspended access cradles and platforms

Background

Classification

CAWS Group A, **CEWS** Class A, **CI/SfB** Code (--)(A5)

Read the Introduction (page 9) before using the following guidelines

Scope

- Structure mass/site plan - restrictions imposed by adjacent buildings/land use.
- Site topography - alignment, stability, level, slope, terrain, groundwater.
- Site ergonomics - traffic routes, movements, personnel, plant, machinery, materials.
- Site entrances/exits - pedestrian, vehicular, site lines.
- Site security, prevention of flooding, interface with occupiers, other trades.
- Services, fuel storage - electricity, water oil, gas, overhead/underground.
- Plant layout/routes - tower cranes, mobiles/position, reach.
- Site accommodation - location of, and access to welfare, site storage layout.
- Emergency access/first aid - accommodation, facilities, staff.

Exclusions

- Specialist areas
  - Nuclear installations
  - Floating facilities
  - Petro-chemical works
  - Quarries
  - Airfields (Active).

Major Hazards

Refer to the Introduction (page 9) for details of accident types and health risks

Struck by mobile plant
Impact, crushing, slipping, falling, two way traffic, working cranes.

Static machinery
Inadequate protection and alerts to static machines operating.

Electrical shock, fire, explosion
Location of site services, temporary, permanent storage of flammable gases, liquids.

Falling from height
Falling from structure or falling into excavation.

Impact, crushing
Objects falling from height from insecure location, work overhead, delivery and storage, unstable structures.

Poor visibility
Layout of access, roads, accommodation work area, people and material movers.

A5 GENERAL PLANNING

B EXCAVATIONS AND FOUNDATIONS

C PRIMARY STRUCTURE

D BUILDING ELEMENTS AND BUILDING SERVICES

E CIVIL ENGINEERING

Specific Hazard Identification

Possible considerations:

- **Sequence** - What is the proposed sequence of construction?
- **Layout** - Ensure site layout proposals reflect the construction sequence. Has it been reviewed since last process change?
- **Phased access** - Is there adequate access onto site throughout all phases of the work?
- **Interfaces** - Where have access routes for plant and personnel been defined for each phase? Separation?
- **Services protection** - Define routes and protection for temporary and permanent site services.
- **Site storage** - Where is there adequate allowance for site storage?
- **Welfare** - Where is there space for welfare facilities and site offices?
- **Cranage** - What are the proposals for location of cranes?
- **Security** - What is site work area security during work activities for operatives?
- **Any others?**

Prompts

- Plant and machinery
- Vehicle/Pedestrians
- Sequence of construction
- Storage
- Welfare accommodation
- Access - temporary/permanent - vertical/horizontal
- Services (temp/permanent)
- Cranage (vertical movement)
- Conveyance (horizontal movement)
- Site access roads
- Temporary works
- Control measures
- Emergency services
- Fire prevention
- Fire-fighting
- Adjacent occupiers

Hazards Consideration in Design

Stage	Considerations and issues	Possible design options to avoid or mitigate hazards identified for site layout
Concept Design	• Why this layout? • Vehicle/Pedestrian Separation • Site ergonomics • Block location • Project phasing • Emergency provision • Major movements • Facilities locations • System layout	• Is the site and/or its layout conducive for: - mechanical or manual construction? - off-site fabrication rather than insitu? - off site storage preferred to on-site? • Ensure the site layout can accommodate labour and plant necessary to complete the work on time. • Site access roads - one-way roads safer. • Prepare site layouts to reduce construction activities on site and therefore reduce risks.
Scheme Design	• System phasing • Welfare facilities • Deliveries/access • Storage layout • Handling methods • Major services • Element layout	• Design of phased completion to allow continued safe construction and occupation of finished work, if required. • Consider width, height, load constraints for access to the work face. • Having decided on site layout for construction access, ensure maintenance access is also adequate.
Detail Design	• Working space • Trade separation • Routing services • Positioning element • Identify services • Surveying	• Design to allow use of permanent roads as site roads. • Ensure minimum number of handling activities created by the design. • Avoid design sequence causing different trades to have to work together. • Design service routes to avoid active construction.

Examples of Risk Mitigation (methods of solution)

ACTION \ ISSUE	Site layout logic	Traffic movement
Avoidance Design to avoid identified hazards but beware of introducing others	Plan site strategy/ergonomics. Phasing of site layouts with phased completion.	Road layout. Location on site.
Reduction Design to reduce identified hazards but beware of increasing others	Sequence each construction discipline.	Transportation study. Site road layout to be considered.
Control Design to provide acceptable safeguards for all remaining identified hazards	Consider site disciplines necessary. Identify site hazards created.	Site traffic procedures.

Examples of Risk Mitigation (issues addressed at different stages)

A terraced building in a city street is to be demolished and rebuilt. There are extensive parking restrictions in the area and the contractor will not be able to off-load materials or plant outside the site perimeter. There is no space available for unloading between the site perimeter and the proposed building.

Concept design	Scheme design	Detail design
Temporary vehicle access will be designed into the new building as part of temporary works to reduce hazards.	The design will improve access by omitting part of the first floor during construction, allowing off-street delivery and unloading.	Omit two bays of structure at first floor level, with ground floor structure able to carry site vehicles as temporary access area.

A 1960s office block is to be extensively refurbished. The existing heating systems are to be replaced with full air-conditioning and the concrete cladding units are to be replaced with insulated aluminium and glass cladding. The office must be kept operational as far as possible, consistent with the extensive refurbishment.

Concept design	Scheme design	Detail design
Options reviewed indicate hazard reduction with a full structural scaffold to carry out building refurbishment works, despite the restriction the scaffold imposes on site layout.	The facade scaffold layout will be designed to be amended to follow the refurbishment programme of activities and provide temporary support for the replacement of cladding units.	Design of structural scaffold to span access into the building loading bays for delivery vehicles to avoid unloading in the site area.

GENERAL PLANNING — A 5

EXCAVATIONS AND FOUNDATIONS — B

PRIMARY STRUCTURE — C

BUILDING ELEMENTS AND BUILDING SERVICES — D

CIVIL ENGINEERING — E

Related Issues

References within this document

References	Related issues
A1	Surrounding environment could influence decisions on site layout.
A2	Site clearance will facilitate site layout planning.
A4	Access onto the site will be an integral part of the plan for the site layout.
B1-B3	Excavation will cause sequential implementation of site layout.
B4-7	Foundations as an early activity will determine site layout.
C1-C4	The supply of concrete and the installation of concrete structures will determine site layout.
C5-C6	Structural steel members, if significant in size and quantity will affect site layout.
D1	External cladding delivery and installation will interact with site layout.
E2	Roads integral/adjacent to the site will have a determining effect on site layout.
E3	Railways and their safety requirements are likely to affect site layout.

References for Further Guidance

Primary general references and background information given in Section 4

Primary

- HSE(G)47 Avoiding danger from underground services
- HSE GS5 Entry into confined spaces
- HSE HS(G)141 Electricity on construction sites
- HSE GS6 Avoidance of danger from overhead electric lines

Secondary

- Building Employers Confederation Fire prevention on construction sites; Joint Code of Practice
- HSE(G)32 Safety in falsework for in-situ beams and slabs
- HSE HS(G)66 Protection of workers and the general public during development on contaminated land
- HSE IND(G)148L Reversing Vehicles
- CIRIA Special Publication 78 Building on Derelict Land 1991
- CIRIA Special Publication 57 Handling of materials on site 1988
- CIRIA DM043 Site Organisation and Planning (Video 6)
- DoT, Interdepartmental Committee on the Redevelopment of Contaminated Land (ICRCL) Guidance note 17/78 Notes on the development and After-use of land-fill sites 1990

Background

- CIRIA Special Publication 38 - Simple noise screens for site use 1985

Classification

CAWS Group A,   **CEWS** Class A,   **CI/SfB** Code (--)(A5)

Read the Introduction (page 9) before using the following guidelines

Scope

Excavations for:

- Foundations - buildings structures (bridges, retaining walls).
- Trenches - services, drainage, walls.
- Earthwork cuttings - road works, railways, services, water courses, minerals.
- Basements/shafts - buildings, drainage, services.
- Pits - ponds, waste disposal, archaeology.
- Heritage sites.

Exclusions

- Cofferdams and caissons - work adjacent to deep water, working in compressed air (see E7).
- Tunnels.
- Unexploded bombs.

Major Hazards

Refer to the Introduction (page 9) for details of accident types and health risks

Buried/crushed/trapped
Collapse of insufficiently supported sides of excavation. Undermining adjacent structures.

Falls
People, objects, supports, plant/machinery, materials. Unauthorised access.

Plant and machinery
Crushed/trapped/hit by plant falling/running into excavation. Fumes (e.g. carbon monoxide).

Intrusive occurrences
Groundwater, sewage, flooding. Fire, explosion, smoke, gas leakage, methane

Health hazards
Contaminated ground/water.
Toxic chemicals.
Asbestos.
Microbiological diseases.
Dust and allergens.
Skin irritants.

Services
Electrocution.
Gas pipelines.
Sewage and process effluents.

GENERAL PLANNING | A

EXCAVATIONS AND FOUNDATIONS | B1

PRIMARY STRUCTURE | C

BUILDING ELEMENTS AND BUILDING SERVICES | D

CIVIL ENGINEERING | E

A — GENERAL PLANNING

B1 — EXCAVATIONS AND FOUNDATIONS

C — PRIMARY STRUCTURE

D — BUILDING ELEMENTS AND BUILDING SERVICES

E — CIVIL ENGINEERING

Specific Hazard Identification

Possible key considerations:

- **Site survey** - What are site conditions?
- **Ground Investigation** - Water table and slope stability?
- **Surface water** - What is local topography? Where are rivers, lakes, canals, ponds, etc.?
- **Working space** - What plant is required for backfilling?
- **Stockpile/disposal** - What are length and location of temporary roads and traffic routes to tip?
- **Adjacent property** - What are the position, type and use?
- **Services** - Where are they located?
- **Any others?**

Prompts

- Historical records
- Archaeology
- Contaminated land
- Waterborne diseases
- Access/egress
- Existing outfalls and vents
- Environment: general public, weather, buildings
- Working procedures

Hazards Consideration in Design

Stage	Considerations and issues	Possible design options to avoid or mitigate hazards identified for general excavation
Concept Design		• An investigation of local earthworks could identify suitable minimum excavation site slopes. • Design to avoid possibility of excavation undermining adjacent buildings. • Consider possible locations of hard routes and tip sites to have least effect on construction and local community. • Ensure that ground investigation will detect likely site-specific contamination. • The ground investigation should relate to a range of option designs for the proposed structure.
Scheme Design	• Why excavate? • Structure location and layout • Site history • Materials • Ground investigation • Adjacent structure details • Watercourses • Disposal of excavated materials • Services • Slope stability • Working space • Waste disposal/haul routes • Stabilise excavation • Drainage	• In low-lying waterlogged ground, consider dewatering methods to stabilise excavations. • For sites with limited working space, consider excavation within piled supports. • Assess risk of diverting services versus alternative of working around them.
Detail Design		• For bored pile side supports in contaminated ground, consider handling and disposal of spoil. • Consider shoring options for adjacent structure, to maximise working space within site excavation. • Consider surface water drainage system to mitigate flooding of excavation.

Examples of Risk Mitigation (methods of solution)

ISSUE ACTION	Flooding	Unstable ground
Avoidance Design to avoid identified hazards but beware of introducing others	Raise level of building.	Stabilise ground.
Reduction Design to reduce identified hazards but beware of increasing others	Change foundation design from pads to piles.	Minimise depth of excavation. Batter side slopes.
Control Design to provide acceptable safeguards for all remaining identified hazards	Consider grout curtain, well-pointing or other drainage.	Outline appropriate propping requirements.

*Side tabs: GENERAL PLANNING **A** | EXCAVATIONS AND FOUNDATIONS **B1** | PRIMARY STRUCTURE **C** | BUILDING ELEMENTS AND BUILDING SERVICES **D** | CIVIL ENGINEERING **E***

Examples of Risk Mitigation (issues addressed at different stages)

Buildings are to be demolished within an urban environment to provide a new shopping arcade with basement car parking. Neighbouring buildings abut the development site. There must be agreed and acceptable methods of work to prevent the collapse of excavations and buildings.

Concept design	Scheme design	Detail design
Identify history of site. Provide fully engineered retaining wall(s).	Consider new/existing structure interface and possible demolition/excavation techniques. Stability of excavation paramount. Restrict horizontal wall movements.	Retaining walls left in place for the underground car park. Consider additional methods of wall stabilisation, permanent or temporary. Consider access needs for construction and of local populace during the works.

A proposed leisure centre is to be constructed on stable made-up ground. The proposed excavation for foundations and services could be in contaminated ground.

Concept design	Scheme design	Detail design
Obtain historical records/surveys of site, detailing extent of contamination, from client. Avoid excavation in areas of known toxicity. Locate services in areas where there is no contamination, if possible.	Avoid contact with contaminants. Reduce contact by design of capping layer or use of driven piles to minimise ground disturbance. Test for types of waste product.	Consider implications for unavoidable works in contaminated area and provide relevant information to the Planning Supervisor. Put services in ducts to minimise future ground disturbance.

Group B - Excavations and foundations
1 - General excavation

Related Issues

References within this document

References	Related issues
A1	Local environment should be protected from the hazards associated with excavations. OH + UG services may need diversion, temporary support or protection. Adjacent structures (including walls) may need temporary support, additional support (shoring), underpinning, etc.
A2	Demolition could precede excavation. Locate the health and safety file.
A3	Ground investigations should include testing for toxic materials, soil density, gasses, stability and groundwater details.
A4	Access/egress routes should be suitable for emergency services and for assumed construction plant.
A5	Site layout should be related to the working space available, the excavation plant to be used and the size of the site.
B2	- deep basements and shafts
B3	- trenches for foundations and services
B4	- retaining walls
E1	Working space availability on a small site accentuates the hazards of excavation. Careful planning is required.
E2,E3	Excavation adjacent to roads and railways should include for safe clearance distances.
E6,E7	Working near water introduces a greater risk that the excavation may flood.
	For issues associated with specific excavation work, refer to other sections in this group, e.g.:

References for Further Guidance

Primary general references and background information given in Section 4

Primary

- CIRIA Report 97 Trenching practice 1992
- CIRIA Report 130 Methane: its occurrence and hazards in construction 1993
- HSE HS(G) 47 Avoiding danger from underground services
- HSE HS(G) 66 Protection of workers and the general public during the development of contaminated land
- HSE CIS8 (revised) Safety in excavations
- HSE GS5 Entry into confined spaces

Secondary

- HSE GS6 Avoidance of danger from overhead electric lines
- HSE GS29 Parts 1 to 4 Health and safety in demolition work

Background

- BS 6031:1981 Code of practice for Earthworks
- BS 8002:1994 Earth Retaining Structures

Classification

CAWS   Group D,   **CEWS**   Class E,   **CI/SfB**   Code (1-)C

Group B - Excavations and foundations
2 - Deep basements and shafts

B2

Read the Introduction (page 9) before using the following guidelines

Scope

- Basements for buildings, multi-storey offices, residential block, warehouses, car parks, etc.
- Large diameter access shafts (diameters greater than 3 metres).

Exclusions

- Piles up to 3 metres diameter (see B6).
- Shafts for mining industry.
- Cofferdams (see E7)

Major Hazards

Refer to the Introduction (page 9) for details of accident types and health risks

Falls
Falling into excavation or shaft. Debris or materials dropped into shaft or excavation.

Buried/crushed/trapped
Excavation collapse due to lack of or insufficient support.

Health hazards
Contaminated ground and water.

Services
Gas pipelines.
Electrocution.
Flooding by water or effluent.

Ground effects
Sudden inrush or ground water.
Mudslides.
Artesian boiling.
Methane.

Plant and machinery
Crushed/trapped/hit by plant in excavation.
Liquid fuels and exhaust fumes.

A — GENERAL PLANNING

B2 — EXCAVATIONS AND FOUNDATIONS

C — PRIMARY STRUCTURE

D — BUILDING ELEMENTS AND BUILDING SERVICES

E — CIVIL ENGINEERING

A — GENERAL PLANNING

B2 — EXCAVATIONS AND FOUNDATIONS

C — PRIMARY STRUCTURE

D — BUILDING ELEMENTS AND BUILDING SERVICES

E — CIVIL ENGINEERING

Specific Hazard Identification

Possible key considerations:

- **Site survey** - Where are adjacent structures and services located?
- **Ground investigation** - What condition is soil, what is water table level?
- **Hydrology** - Where are water courses and aquifers?
- **Gases** - What level of ventilation is required?
- **Working space** - What is required for working ramps, stockpiling, deliveries of machinery?
- **Supports** - What systems will be appropriate?
- **Technological developments** - How can these be incorporated?
- **Any others?**

Prompts

- Historical records
- Archaeology
- Contaminated land
- Waterborne diseases
- Access/egress
- Existing outfalls and vents
- Environment: general public, weather, buildings
- Working procedures

Hazards Consideration in Design

Stage	Considerations and issues	Possible design options to avoid or mitigate hazards identified for deep basements and shafts
Concept Design		• On the basis of site investigation, determine excavation methods to be excluded and identify hazardous materials and ground water problems to be addressed. • Consider excavation proposals to minimise the effects on overhead and underground services or divert services either temporarily or permanently. • Consider excavation within contiguous bored piles which will form permanent walls (e.g. for a basement). • Ensure ground investigation confirms the extent and type of any contamination.
Scheme Design	• Why excavate? • Structure location and layout • Site history • Materials • Ground investigation • Adjacent structure details • Watercourses • Disposal of excavated materials • Services • Slope stability • Working space • Waste disposal/haul routes • Stabilise excavation • Drainage	• Ensure ground investigation confirms the extent and type of any contamination. • Excavation must not compromise the structural integrity of adjacent buildings. (Consider effects on ground stability.) • Design to take into account working space available and effects on local environment.
Detail Design		• Support details should be sufficient to contain or exclude contaminants. • For excluded material, consider safe methods of disposal. • Appropriate sharing techniques of adjacent buildings need to be identified (e.g. ground anchors). • Design to identify appropriate practical and safe temporary access. • Designer's assumptions on construction, sequence and methods to be identified in health and safety plan. • Organise advance diversion of services by the service provider.

Group B - Excavations and foundations
2 - Deep basements and shafts

Examples of Risk Mitigation (methods of solution)

ACTION	Collapse	Methane from the ground
Avoidance Design to avoid identified hazards but beware of introducing others	Design for shaft construction and inspection using remote control methods (e.g. robotics).	Incorporation of a gas - impermeable membrane is the first construction activity.
Reduction Design to reduce identified hazards but beware of increasing others	Assume mechanical excavation only, with operator in safety cab at all times.	Install continuous mechanical ventilation.
Control Design to provide acceptable safeguards for all remaining identified hazards	Manual operations to be easy and of short duration, within the protected area.	Ventilation system activated by gas sensor

ISSUE

Examples of Risk Mitigation (issues addressed at different stages)

Part of a railway terminus is to be sold for property development.
The site contains an abandoned shaft and connecting tunnels which must be isolated from tunnels still in use.

Concept design	Scheme design	Detail design
Consider condition of shaft and possible re-use, as alternatives to backfilling.	Does isolation require local breakage and removal of the tunnel linings, or will substantial "plugs" be sufficient?	Check that there is a sequence of filling which keeps escape routes open and minimises depth of uncured/fluid backfill material.

A bridge construction requires the sinking of vertical shafts to complete the pier foundations. Ground investigation has revealed the presence of hard granite boulders which precludes boring techniques.

Concept design	Scheme design	Detail design
Consider possible and appropriate mechanical and/or manual excavation techniques.	Consider appropriate excavation techniques, related to location, access, topography, ground stability, plant.	Materials disposal, temporary access, stockpile. Protection of personnel in hole - support design.

Related Issues

References within this document

References	Related issues
A1	Local environment should be protected from the hazards associated with excavations. In particular, adjacent structures (including walls) may need temporary support, additional support (shoring), underpinning, etc. Consider also movements of local populace and location of services/utilities.
A3	Ground investigations should include testing for toxic materials from former use, soil density, gases, stability and ground water details.
A4	Access/egress routes should be kept clean, clear of obstructions and be suitable for emergency services.
A5	Site layout should be related to the working space available, the excavation plant to be used and the size of the site.
E1	Working space on small sites accentuate the hazards of excavation.
E2,E3	Excavation adjacent to roads and railways should include safe clearance distances and/or controls for site personnel together with control of excavation traffic.
E6,E7	Working near water introduces a greater risk that the excavation may flood.

References for Further Guidance

Primary general references and background information given in Section 4

Primary

- HSE HS(G) 47 Avoiding danger from underground services
- HSE HS(G) 66 Protection of workers and the general public during the development of contaminated land
- HSE GS5 Entry into confined spaces
- HSE GS6 Avoidance of danger from overhead electric lines
- HSE CIS8 (revised) Safety in excavations
- BS 8008:1996 Guide to safety precautions and procedures for the construction and descent of machine-bored shafts for piling and other purposes

Secondary

- CIRIA Report 139 Water resisting basements 1995

Background

- The Institution of Structural Engineers Code - Design and construction of deep basements
- Tomlinson Foundation design and construction (Longmans)
- BS 8004:1986 Code of practice for foundations
- CIRIA Report 104 Design of retaining walls embedded in stiff clays 1984

Classification

CAWS Group G, **CI/SfB** Code (1-)C

Read the Introduction (page 9) before using the following guidelines

Scope

- Trenches for strip foundations and pad foundations.
- Trenches for public utilities, services, pipe lines, drains, etc.
- Pits and pipe jacking.

Exclusions

- Deep pier foundations, underpinning.
- Trench depths > 6m and below water.
- Trenches adjacent to deep water.

Major Hazards

Refer to the Introduction (page 9) for details of accident types and health risks

Services
Electrocution.
Gas pipelines.
Sewage and process effluents.

Health hazards
Water-borne toxins and diseases.
Methane.
Asbestos.

Inundation
Flooding, drowning.
Chemical waste, effluents.

Plant and machinery
Vehicles too close cause trench side
to collapse.
Fuel vapours and exhaust fumes.
Pneumatic tools (vibration white
finger).

Falls
No guard rails, congested sites, lack
of working space.

Buried/crushed/trapped
Materials/spoil, falls into trench.
Trench collapse due to insufficient
support.

A — GENERAL PLANNING

B3 — EXCAVATIONS AND FOUNDATIONS

C — PRIMARY STRUCTURE

D — BUILDING ELEMENTS AND BUILDING SERVICES

E — CIVIL ENGINEERING

Specific Hazard Identification

Possible key considerations:

- **Site survey** - Where are the services?
- **Services** - Do services need support across trench?
- **General investigation** - What are soil types? What is the water table level? Could the trench flood?
- **Hydrology** - Where are the water courses? Will surface water run-off be a problem?
- **Side supports** - What systems are appropriate for the known ground conditions?
- **Gases** - What assessment is required to decide ventilation?
- **Working space** - What space is required for deliveries, stockpiling, ramps, haul road? Ensure safe distance from trench.
- **Backfilling** - What compaction can be carried out without using hand-held machines?
- **Any others?**

Prompts

- Historical records
- Archaeology (where appropriate)
- Contaminated land
- Protection of public
- Access/egress
- Illumination
- Waste disposal
- Noise/vibration
- Emergency procedures
- Propriety systems
- Confined space working
- Pipe jacking
- Trenchless methods

Hazards Consideration in Design

Stage	Considerations and issues	Possible design options to avoid or mitigate hazards identified for trenches for foundations and services
Concept Design		• Establish details of foundations of existing structures and previous work at the site. • Identify necessary working space in relation to existing buildings and services. • Identify (and reduce) effects on local environment and services. • Look for alternative routes to avoid deep trenches and steeply sloping ground.
Scheme Design	• Why trenches? • Site inspection • Site history • Access/egress • Working space • Environment • Topography • Services • Ground conditions • Contamination • Rights of way • Plant/machinery • Trench supports • Drainage proposals • Adjacent structures • Working procedures	• Establish ground conditions and identify safe working space for excavation depths required. • The presence of water can create instability. Minimise need and depth of excavation. • Consider construction techniques to avoid need for trench excavation (e.g. local excavation and pipe jacking or slit trench and automatic cable laying).
Detail Design		• To minimise effects of water, include for drainage system to restrict/divert ground waste and run-off. • Consider problems of existing services which cross proposed excavation. Identify necessary support systems. • Minimise the time and complexity of manual operations (e.g. jointing) to be carried out in trench.

Group B - Excavations and foundations
3 - Trenches for foundations and services

B3

Examples of Risk Mitigation (methods of solution)

ACTION / ISSUE	Collapse of adjacent foundations	Flooding from adjacent watercourse
Avoidance Design to avoid identified hazards but beware of introducing others	Relocate or use shallower trench or use trenchless construction.	Relocate trench. Do not excavate near watercourse.
Reduction Design to reduce identified hazards but beware of increasing others	Install underpinning or temporary works ahead of trenching.	Redirect watercourse, reinforce banks, extend flood defences.
Control Design to provide acceptable safeguards for all remaining identified hazards	Monitor movement and specify that appropriate plant and materials always to be available.	Allow for the early construction of an appropriate system of drains and pumps.

Examples of Risk Mitigation (issues addressed at different stages)

A communications company wants to provide the option of cable TV to all properties in a township of historical interest.

Concept design	Scheme design	Detail design
Can the existing telephone cable network be used? Is there major work planned by other communication/utility companies?	Consider trench sharing with other services. Keep away from existing services and use combined dig-and-lay techniques.	Programme the works to avoid bad weather, local events, and tourist seasons.

A two-storey townhouse is to be constructed in an urban setting. Properties are located on each side and to the rear. The site has a road frontage.
Excavation for strip footing foundations is in topsoil/clay.

Concept design	Scheme design	Detail design
Layout to consider ground slope, services location, access. Consider also adjacent buildings/structures.	Consider stepped footings on sloping ground. Services, water table, stockpile of excavated material.	Stepped footings reduce excavated depth. Drainage measures to reduce flooding risk. Plant location during concreting. Use concrete backfill to reduce settlement.

GENERAL PLANNING — A

EXCAVATIONS AND FOUNDATIONS — B3

PRIMARY STRUCTURE — C

BUILDING ELEMENTS AND BUILDING SERVICES — D

CIVIL ENGINEERING — E

A GENERAL PLANNING

B3 EXCAVATIONS AND FOUNDATIONS

C PRIMARY STRUCTURE

D BUILDING ELEMENTS AND BUILDING SERVICES

E CIVIL ENGINEERING

Related Issues

References within this document

References	Related issues
A1	Local environment should be protected from the hazards associated with excavations. Identify also location of services/building utilities.
A3	Ground investigations should include testing for toxic materials, soil density, gases, stability and ground water details.
A4	Access/egress routes should be kept clean, clear of obstructions and be suitable for emergency services.
A5	Site layout should be related to the working space available, designer's assumptions of excavation plant to be used and the size of the site.
E1	Working space on small sites accentuates the hazards of excavation. Consider practicalities of excavation and construction sequence.
E2,E3	Excavation adjacent to roads and railways should include safe clearance distances and/or suitable protection for site personnel.
E6,E7	Working near water introduces a greater risk that the excavation may flood.

References for Further Guidance

Primary general references and background information given in Section 4

Primary

- CIRIA Report 97 Trenching practice 1992
- CIRIA Technical Note 127 Trenchless construction for underground services 1987
- HSE CIS8 (revised) Safety in excavations
- DOT Safety at streetworks and roadworks: A Code of Practice, 1992

Secondary

- HSE HS(G) 47 Avoiding danger from underground services
- HSE HS(G) 66 Protection of workers and the general public during the development of contaminated land
- HSE GS5 Entry into confined spaces
- HSE GS6 Avoidance of danger from overhead electric lines
- CIRIA Funders Report CP/12 Trenchless and minimum excavation technology: Planning and investigation

Background

- CIRIA Report 130 Methane: its occurrence and hazards in construction 1993
- CIRIA Technical Note 112 Pipe jacking: a state-of-the-art review 1983

Classification

CAWS	Group D,P&R	**CEWS**	Classes E,I,J,K,L&Z	**CI/SfB**	Code (1-)C

Read the Introduction (page 9) before using the following guidelines

Scope

- Single-storey basements, drainage chambers, service ducts.
- Earthworks/cuttings: roadworks, railways, watercourses, landscaping.
- Temporary retaining walls, e.g. sheet piles.

Exclusions

- Deep basements and shafts (see B2).
- Cofferdams and caissons (see E7).
- Mining and work adjacent to deep water.
- Gabions.

Major Hazards

Refer to the Introduction (page 9) for details of accident types and health risks

Buried/crushed/trapped
Collapse of unretained material.
Collapse of incomplete and
temporarily unstable wall.
Inadequate working space behind wall.

Falls
Into base excavation from top of
incomplete wall.
Into water-filled excavation or
temporarily-retained water.

Plant and transport
Site traffic. Slewing of concrete skip,
shutters, etc.
Work adjacent to road/railway.

Services
Electrocution.
Gas pipelines.
Sewage and process effluents.
Emergency. communications.

Ground movements
Subsidence of adjacent structures.
Fractured services and waste pipes.

Health hazards
Noise/vibration.
Dust inhalation.
Fumes.
Water-borne diseases.
Manual handling.

A GENERAL PLANNING

B 4 EXCAVATIONS AND FOUNDATIONS

C PRIMARY STRUCTURE

D BUILDING ELEMENTS AND BUILDING SERVICES

E CIVIL ENGINEERING

Specific Hazard Identification

Possible key considerations:

- **Site survey** - Where are service? What structures are adjacent to site? What is topography?
- **Ground investigation** - Is there evidence of earth movement? Where is water table?
- **Environment** - What are implications of site location? (e.g. urban, rural, next to river, railway, road).
- **Retaining wall** - What is wall to be used for? What type is it to be (e.g. gravity, reinforced concrete, temporary)?
- **Plant & Machinery** - What is sufficient working space for the proposed construction methods?
- **Sequences** - What are the construction sequences?
- **Access** - What access is required to rear of wall?
- **Any others?**

Prompts

- Soil types
- Services
- Adjacent structures (foundations)
- Retaining wall type
- Plant/machinery
- Access/working space
- Weather
- Backfilling

Hazards Consideration in Design

Stage	Considerations and issues	Possible design options to avoid or mitigate hazards identified for retaining walls
Concept Design	• Why retaining wall? • Location • Environment • Topography • Access	• Position could determine wall type that can be practically and safely constructed: examine options available. • Consider type of wall to minimise hazard of interaction with services, particularly gas and electricity. • Evaluate possible effects on adjacent structures during operation.
Scheme Design	• Services • Wall position • Protection of property • Adjacent structures • Working space • Temporary roads • Ground investigation • Retaining wall types • Plant/machinery • Backfilling • Drainage • Ground stability	• Design to minimise depth of excavations (e.g. incorporate a piled base or grout curtain). • Consider excavation techniques in relation to ground conditions, working space and environmental constraints. (Relate to wall design.) • Identify necessary ground and surface water control systems. • Eliminate need for operatives to access rear of wall in confined spaces. • Backfilling prohibited or limited until a certain stage of wall construction.
Detail Design	• Maintenance • Advance works • Temporary live loads during construction	• Consider temporary diversion of services during retaining wall construction. • Wall design to include facilities for ease of maintenance. • Prefabricated units to provide fixing locations for permanent or temporary guard rails.

Examples of Risk Mitigation (methods of solution)

ACTION \ ISSUE	Ground slippage	Gas pipes crossing line of wall
Avoidance Design to avoid identified hazards but beware of introducing others	Pre-stabilise ground.	Change route of wall to avoid gas pipes.
Reduction Design to reduce identified hazards but beware of increasing others	Consider piles, soil nailing, ground anchors.	Change design of wall in vicinity of gas pipes (e.g. change ground levels or select shallower and wider base).
Control Design to provide acceptable safeguards for all remaining identified hazards	Outline possible staged construction sequence.	Specify robust protection to be incorporated into the permanent works.

Examples of Risk Mitigation (issues addressed at different stages)

An existing busy urban road is to be widened. Land is not available either side. The widening is therefore to be completed on line. The existing cutting slope will require a retaining wall (height 5 metres).

Concept design	Scheme design	Detail design
Consider environmentally appropriate solutions and proposals for existing road traffic. Site history - slope stability.	Bored piles reduce excavation hazard and noise and effects on existing traffic; locate services.	Access/egress site details. Allow for temporary diversion of traffic/ lane closures.

A building is to be constructed within an urban environment. Car parking is to be made available in the basement. The surrounding properties are shops, offices, residential blocks.

Concept design	Scheme design	Detail design
Consider proximity of adjacent properties and road traffic. Relate to environment and location. Noise and vibration issues.	Consider constructing a retaining wall prior to basement excavation. Ground investigation (water-bearing strata). Consider diaphragm wall, combined with ground anchors.	Precast panels/in-situ concrete (underpin adjacent building).

Sidebar tabs:
A — GENERAL PLANNING
B4 — EXCAVATIONS AND FOUNDATIONS
C — PRIMARY STRUCTURE
D — BUILDING ELEMENTS AND BUILDING SERVICES
E — CIVIL ENGINEERING

A GENERAL PLANNING

B4 EXCAVATIONS AND FOUNDATIONS

C PRIMARY STRUCTURE

D BUILDING ELEMENTS AND BUILDING SERVICES

E CIVIL ENGINEERING

Related Issues

References within this document

References	Related issues
A1	Local environment should be protected from the hazards associated with excavations.
A3	Ground investigation should include tests for toxic materials, soil density, gases, stability and groundwater details.
A4	Access/egress routes should be kept clean, clear of obstructions and be suitable for emergency services .
A5	Site layout should be related to the working space available, the excavation plant to be used and the size of the site.
E1	Working space on small sites accentuates the hazards of excavation.
E2,E3	Excavation adjacent to roads and railways should include safe clearance distances and/or suitable protection for site personnel.
E6,E7	Working near water introduces a greater risk that the excavation may flood.
B5	Ground stabilisation may provide a safer solution.
	Underground/overhead services need to be carefully considered.

References for Further Guidance

Primary general references and background information given in Section 4

Primary

- HSE GS5 Entry into confined spaces
- HSE GS6 Avoidance of danger from overhead lines
- HSE GS29 Parts 1 to 4 Health and safety in demolition work
- HSE CIS8 (revised) Safety in excavations
- DOT Safety at Streetworks and Roadworks; A Code of Practice 1993
- CIRIA Report 104 Design of retaining walls embedded in stiff clay 1984

Secondary

- HSE HS(G) 47 Avoiding danger from underground services
- HSE HS(G) 66 Protection of workers and the general public during the development of contaminated land

Background

- BS 8002: 1994 Earth Retaining Structures
- BS8006: 1995 Code of Practice for strengthened/reinforced soils and other fills

Classification

CAWS Group E, **CEWS** Classes E,F&H, **CI/SfB** Code (16)

Read the Introduction (page 9) before using the following guidelines

Scope

- Vibroflotation (vibrocompaction, vibroreplacement).
- Dynamic compaction.
- Lime and cement stabilisation.
- Dewatering/band drains.
- Preloading.
- Jet grouting, permeation grouting (to improve bearing capacity).

Exclusions

- Ground freezing.
- Stabilisation of rock masses (rock bolting, etc.).
- Slope stabilisation (soil nailing, retaining structures, etc.).
- Settlement reducing/elimination measures (e.g. compensation grouting).

Major Hazards

Refer to the Introduction (page 9) for details of accident types and health risks

Plant instability
Inadequate working platform - consider bearing capacity, gradient, stability of fill (settlement), slope stability.

Crushed/trapped
Manoeuvring and slewing of heavy plant and equipment.

Working environment
Noise, vibration, fumes, asphyxiation (e.g. nitrogen), high pressure lines and hoses.

Services
Buried underground and overhead services including gas, electricity, water. Damage by drilling, driving, impact, vibration, settlement.

Health hazards
Contact with contaminated arisings/groundwater.
Dust and irritation from materials (e.g. cement and lime).

Falls
From plant and machinery tilted by uneven/soft ground.

A GENERAL PLANNING

B5 EXCAVATIONS AND FOUNDATIONS

C PRIMARY STRUCTURE

D BUILDING ELEMENTS AND BUILDING SERVICES

E CIVIL ENGINEERING

Specific Hazard Identification

Possible key considerations:

- **Access** - What provisions are necessary at each location?
- **Working space** - What needs to be provided?
- **Working platform** - Where and what is needed?
- **Services** - Where are they located?
- **Stability** - What considerations need to be made for nearby structures?
- **Workers/public** - What is their proximity?
- **Workers** - What is proximity of workers during operations?
- **Contamination** - Where is affected ground and water?
- **Materials** - What substances are hazardous to health?
- **Any others?**

Prompts

- Access routes
- Plant size and weight
- Site survey rig details
- Services check
- Structural survey
- Noise/dust/lifting materials
- Site investigation

Hazards Consideration in Design

Stage	Considerations and issues	Possible design options to avoid or mitigate hazards identified for ground stabilisation
Concept Design		• Review reasons for stabilising (e.g. bearing capacity or settlement). • Identify constraints and consider relocation of structure. • Consider alternative types of structure, such as flexible foundations. • Surveys/site investigation/desk study to enable options to be assessed systematically.
Scheme Design	• Why stabilise? • Location of structure • Overall programme • Type of structure • Surveys/site investigation/desk study • Access • Programme/sequences • Interfaces • Specific alternatives • Depth of stabilisation • Type of stabilisation material • Access/haul routes • Working platform	• Consider access requirements and location relative to public. • Eliminate interface constraints. • Consider alternative stabilisation methods? (Contact experienced specialist contractors for advice.)
Detail Design		• Consider depths of treatment required by design, in relation to plant capabilities (e.g. can smaller plant be used?) • Can an alternative stabilisation material be used (e.g. cement instead of lime)? • Can same access points and haul roads be used throughout contract? • Can working platform form part of permanent works?

Group B - Excavations and foundations
5 - Ground stabilisation

Examples of Risk Mitigation (methods of solution)

ACTION / ISSUE	Use of surcharging	Use of lime piles
Avoidance Design to avoid identified hazards but beware of introducing others	Avoid stabilisation by phased construction (e.g. allow periods for the ground to consolidate between defined stages of construction).	Avoid hazard of lime piles by using stone columns?
Reduction Design to reduce identified hazards but beware of increasing others	Consider preloading or drainage to induce settlement.	Minimise depth of ground treatment to allow lighter/smaller plant to be used?
Control Design to provide acceptable safeguards for all remaining identified hazards	Outline appropriate monitoring locations and criteria. Change the building/structure performance specification for movement.	Outline hazards of plant instability and need to design working platform.

Examples of Risk Mitigation (issues addressed at different stages)

A haul road at a supermarket site is to be constructed on a wet clay subgrade, to enable use of road lorries/tippers. To save on granular material, it is proposed to stabilise the clay subgrade using quick-lime.

Concept design	Scheme design	Detail design
Consider re-aligning haul road and the use of all terrain dump trucks.	To avoid hazard of anhydrous quick-lime, consider alternative forms of stabilisation, e.g. a) Geogrid reinforced, granular roadway with geotextile separation membrane. b) Re-sequence earthmoving to summer period.	To reduce risk associated with exposure to quick-lime, specify lime graded between 3mm and 12mm (to reduce dusting).

An embankment adjacent to an estuary is to be founded on soft clay. It is proposed that vibro-replacement with stone columns will be used to reduce settlement of the embankment.

Concept design	Scheme design	Detail design
To avoid hazard of plant instability, consider re-locating embankment onto stronger ground or the use of lightweight fill to reduce loading.	To avoid hazard of heavy plant (70 tonne) operating on soft material, consider differential and total settlement criteria to see if a shallow foundation type can be adopted (eg. geocell mattress/raft).	Consider using smaller plant. Outline need to plan/sequence work carefully (e.g. work along embankment using stone columns to act as foundation to haul road and working platform for vibroreplacement plant). Separate public and workers from haul road (reroute footpaths)

Related Issues

References within this document

References	Related issues
A1	Surrounding environment will be affected by ground stabilisation work.
A2	Site clearance works may be able to accommodate access provision for future stabilisation work.
A3	Site investigation will be necessary to determine the criteria for future stabilisation work.
A4	Access onto the site will be necessary for the plant.
A5	Site layout determines the extent of the stabilisation necessary.
B1	General excavation may require the use of stabilisation measures.
E2	Working near roads may be undertaken while road is in use.
E3	Working near railways may be undertaken while railway is in use.
E6,E7	Working near water may be a major consideration.
	Contamination may be caused by ground treatment processes (e.g. groundwater).

References for Further Guidance

Primary general references and background information given in Section 4

Primary

- CIRIA Special Publication 123 Soil reinforcement with geotextiles 1995
- CIRIA Book 11 Prefabricated vertical drains 1991
- CIRIA Project Report 10 The design of pore pressure control systems in fine soils 1993
- CIRIA Report 95 Health and safety aspects of ground treatment materials 1982
- ICE Works Construction Guide "Ground stabilisation, deep compaction and grouting"

Secondary

- CIRIA Report 113 Control of groundwater for temporary works 1988
- HSE CIS8 (revised) Safety in excavations

Background

- Construction Industry Training Board CITB/FPS Safety on piling sites
- CIRIA Special Publication 136 Site guide to construction of foundations 1996

Classification

CAWS Group D, **CEWS** Classes E&C, **CI/SfB** Code (11)

Read the Introduction (page 9) before using the following guidelines

Scope

- Foundation piles - bored, driven, timber, steel, concrete.
- Load testing of piles.
- Shafts < 3m diameter.
- Installation of sheet piles.

Exclusions

- Piles for underpinning (see B7).
- Piling over water (see E6).
- Piling next to railways and/or roads (see E2, E3).

Major Hazards

Refer to the Introduction (page 9) for details of accident types and health risks

Plant instability
Inadequate working platform for equipment - considerations such as: bearing capacity, gradient, stability, variability of ground conditions.

Plant and Machinery
Lifting, slewing and pitching of casings, piles and reinforcement cages. Movement of piling rigs, Delivery of materials.

Working environment
Noise, vibration, exhaust fumes, trips, open bores/excavations, impact from spoil falling off auger.

Services
Buried underground and overhead services including gas, electricity, water and drainage by drilling, driving, impact, vibration, settlement.

Health hazards
Contact with contaminated arisings/groundwater.
Dust and irritation from materials (e.g. bentonite and cement).

Collapse of excavation
Insufficient support of bores/excavation results in collapse, including loss of slimy support materials (e.g. drains). Collapse during inspection of pile base, or collapse due to construction delays.

Side tabs: GENERAL PLANNING **A** | EXCAVATIONS AND FOUNDATIONS **B 6** | PRIMARY STRUCTURE **C** | BUILDING ELEMENTS AND BUILDING SERVICES **D** | CIVIL ENGINEERING **E**

A — GENERAL PLANNING

B 6 — EXCAVATIONS AND FOUNDATIONS

C — PRIMARY STRUCTURE

D — BUILDING ELEMENTS AND BUILDING SERVICES

E — CIVIL ENGINEERING

Specific Hazard Identification

Possible key considerations:

- **Access** - What provision is required at each pile location?
- **Working space** - What needs to be provided?
- **Working platform** - Where and what is needed?
- **Services** - Where are they located?
- **Stability** - What considerations need to be made for nearby structure?
- **Workers/public** - What is the proximity?
- **Contamination** - Where is affected ground and water?
- **Materials** - What substances are hazardous to health?
- **Open pile borings** - How will these be protected?
- **Operations** - What sequences will be adopted?
- **Obstructions** - Check for underground structures and for abandoned foundations, works and services.
- **Any others?**

Prompts

- Access routes
- Plant size
- Site survey/rig details
- Services check
- Structural survey
- Noise/dust
- Lifting materials/crane loads
- Site investigation
- Confined space/falling materials

Hazards Consideration in Design

Stage	Considerations and issues	Possible design options to avoid or mitigate hazards identified for piling
Concept Design		• Review the reasons for piling (e.g. bearing capacity or settlement?). • Identify constraints and consider relocation of structure. • Consider alternatives (e.g. shallow foundations, rafts or flexible foundations such as a reinforced soil mattress). • Surveys/site investigation/desk study to enable different options to be assessed systematically).
Scheme Design	• Why is piling required? • Location of structure • Type of structure • Overall programme • Surveys/site investigation/desk study • Access • Programme/sequences • Interfaces • Type of pile • Working platform • Pile length • Obstructions • Programme • Temporary works	• Consider piling techniques to minimise noise and spreading of spoil (if ground contaminated). • Identify access requirements associated with equipment (e.g. overhead power lines and low headroom). • Programme to allow separation of site activities such as trial piling and demolition (programme and interface constraints). • Consider the magnitude and distribution of structural loads in relation to constraints (e.g. low headroom may restrict pile size).
Detail Design		• Consider support of bore. • How will obstructions such as old basements or unforeseen objects be removed if encountered? • Allow sufficient programme time for method (e.g. Continuous Flight Auger (CFA) bored piles are quick to construct).

Examples of Risk Mitigation (methods of solution)

ACTION \ ISSUE	Piling plant on soft ground	Piling near overhead power lines
Avoidance Design to avoid identified hazards but beware of introducing others	Consider alternative foundation to avoid hazard of piling plant.	Avoid piling near power lines.
Reduction Design to reduce identified hazards but beware of increasing others	Use transfer structure to reduce number of piles, and avoid piling in the softest area.	Design alternative forms of foundations.
Control Design to provide acceptable safeguards for all remaining identified hazards	Outline allowable bearing capacity of ground.	Highlight the hazards.

Examples of Risk Mitigation (issues addressed at different stages)

An embankment is to be located beneath overhead electricity lines and adjacent to pylons. It is proposed to use bored cast in-situ concrete piles.

Concept design	Scheme design	Detail design
To avoid hazard of electrocution, consider moving structure or diverting overhead power lines. If this is not possible reconsider design criteria such as differential settlement rather than total settlement.	Design developed using an increased number of smaller piles with a transfer structure. Adopt bored piles rather than driven piles to avoid hazard of pitching piles.	Use tripod rigs/cut down mast on piling rig to enable safety zone to be maintained. Detail pile reinforcement to suit headroom restrictions.

Building layout requires high column loads to be supported. It is proposed to adopt large diameter under-reamed bored piles. Consider hazard of pile bore instability during base inspection.

Concept design	Scheme design	Detail design
Consider a design that uses transfer structures to allow use of more, smaller diameter, straight shafted piles. Carry out trial pile to check underream stability?	Consider use of larger diameter shaft and smaller diameter underream. Consider reducing number of underream piles by having fewer larger diameter piles. Down rate pile base and accept inspection by CCTV. Use base grouting of pile?	Design casing to support pile shaft. Make inspection cage equal in height to uncased height. Specification of unavoidable inspection requirements to favour sampling and testing of the shortest duration possible.

Side tabs: GENERAL PLANNING **A** / EXCAVATIONS AND FOUNDATIONS **B 6** / PRIMARY STRUCTURE **C** / BUILDING ELEMENTS AND BUILDING SERVICES **D** / CIVIL ENGINEERING **E**

Related Issues

References within this document

References	Related issues
A1	Surrounding environment will be affected by piling operations.
A2	Site clearance works should accommodate access provisions for future piling works.
A3	Site investigation will be necessary to determine data for piling work.
A2,A3	Ground contamination will influence choice of piling.
A4	Access requirements for piling equipment is a major consideration.
A5	Site layout may influence piling method.
B1	General excavation requirements may influence piling methods and equipment.
C1,C2	Concrete methods need to be considered.
E2	Working near roads may have to be undertaken while road is in use.
E3	Working near railways is usually undertaken while railway is in use.
E6,E7	Working near water may be a major consideration.
	Underground services are a major factor in piling operations.

References for Further Guidance

Primary general references and background information given in Section 4

Primary

- Construction Industry Training Board CITB/FPS Document GE 708 Safety on piling sites
- BS 8008: 1996 A guide to safety precautions and procedures for the construction and descent of machine bored shafts for piling and other purposes
- CIRIA Piling guide 1 A review of bearing pile types 1988
- CIRIA Special Publication 131 Crane stability on site 1996

Secondary

- CIRIA Piling guides 2 to 9 (some microfiche only)
- HSE CIS 8 (revised) Safety in excavations

Background

- CIRIA Special Publication 105 Remedial treatment for contaminated land, Vol V: Excavation and disposal

Classification

CAWS   Group D,   **CEWS**   Classes O,P,N&Q,   **CI/SfB**   Code (17)

Read the Introduction (page 9) before using the following guidelines

Scope

- Mass concrete underpinning.
- Pier and beam underpinning.
- Pile and beam underpinning.
- Mini-piling.

Exclusions

- Jet grouting and permeation grouting (see B5).

Major Hazards

Refer to the Introduction (page 9) for details of accident types and health risks

Structural instability
Inadequate stability of structure and risk to workers and occupants of the buildings.

Crushed/trapped
Narrow spaces and low headroom for manoeuvring heavy plant and materials. Manual handling of casings, reinforcement, trench sheets and concrete in confined spaces.

Working environment
Noise, vibration, fumes (confined space ventilation?).
Use of tools in confined spaces.

Services
Buried underground services and overhead services including gas, electricity, water inside and outside buildings. Damage by drilling, driving, impact, vibration, settlement.

Health hazards
Contact with contaminated arisings/groundwater, cement, concrete, adhesives, including inhalation of fumes and dusts (e.g. fibres from dry materials).

Collapse of excavations
Insufficient support results in collapse with risk of entrapment or falls and sudden water inflow/flooding.

GENERAL PLANNING — A

EXCAVATIONS AND FOUNDATIONS — B 7

PRIMARY STRUCTURE — C

BUILDING ELEMENTS AND BUILDING SERVICES — D

CIVIL ENGINEERING — E

A GENERAL PLANNING

B 7 EXCAVATIONS AND FOUNDATIONS

C PRIMARY STRUCTURE

D BUILDING ELEMENTS AND BUILDING SERVICES

E CIVIL ENGINEERING

Specific Hazard Identification

Possible key considerations:

- **Access** - What provisions are necessary?
- **Working space** - What needs to be provided?
- **Services** - Where are they located?
- **Stability** - What is the condition of brickwork/walls?
- **Workers/public** - What is the proximity?
- **Contamination** - Where is affected ground and water?
- **Materials** - Where are substances hazardous to health?
- **Manual handling** - What is the extent of this aspect?
- **Hand tools** - What provisions need to be made?
- **Any others?**

Prompts

- Access routes
- Plant size
- Services
- Structural survey
- Noise/dust
- Handling materials
- Site investigation

Hazards Consideration in Design

Stage	Considerations and issues	Possible design options to avoid or mitigate hazards identified for underpinning
Concept Design		• Consider strengthening and/or repair of structure instead of underpinning. • Consider removing cause of distress and repairing structure? • Consider stabilising ground (e.g. grouting old mineworkings). • Structural survey/site investigation/desk study to understand problem systematically.
Scheme Design	• Why underpin? • Type of structure • Access • Interfaces • Surveys/site investigation/desk study • Type of underpinning • Stability during underpinning • Sequences • Handling materials • Work sequences • Detailing • Temporary works • Monitoring	• Choice of shallow foundations may reduce hazard of entrapment. • Choice of mini-piling may reduce excavation of contaminated material. • Excavation may destabilise structure. • Consider mini-piles and needling, which may cause less disturbance to a fragile structure.
Detail Design		• Define sequence of support to avoid instability. • Avoid starter bars. • Require monitoring of structure/ground during work, having defined allowable movements.

Examples of Risk Mitigation (methods of solution)

	ISSUE **Need to underpin**	**Mass concrete underpinning**
ACTION		
Avoidance Design to avoid identified hazards but beware of introducing others	Avoid underpinning by addressing cause of ground movement and repairing structure.	Avoid entrapment by avoiding descent of excavations (remote operation and inspection).
Reduction Design to reduce identified hazards but beware of increasing others	Consider different types of underpinning available and hazards with each.	Reduce hazard of excavation by minimising descent.
Control Design to provide acceptable safeguards for all remaining identified hazards	Outline interface issues (time, space etc). Associated with types of underpinning.	Outline need to control groundwater inflow in H&S Plan.

Side tabs:
- GENERAL PLANNING — A
- EXCAVATIONS AND FOUNDATIONS — B 7
- PRIMARY STRUCTURE — C
- BUILDING ELEMENTS AND BUILDING SERVICES — D
- CIVIL ENGINEERING — E

Examples of Risk Mitigation (issues addressed at different stages)

Structure constructed on varying depth of made ground is to be underpinned.

Concept design	**Scheme design**	**Detail design**
Mass concrete underpinning chosen to avoid hazard of piling plant. Underpinning to be continuous, carried out in a "hit-and-miss" manner.	Consider dowels protruding into "miss" bays/ excavation. Design for use of: - bar couplers/reinforcement coupler strips, or - "joggle/key" joint - smaller diameter mild steel dowel bars (10/12mm diameter) that can be bent out of way.	Choose small diameter dowels. Control hazard by placing "mushroom" caps on projecting dowel bars to protect workers in trenches.

Structure on contaminated ground is to be underpinned.

Concept design	**Scheme design**	**Detail design**
The design is to consider techniques that do not involve excavation. Can the structure be strengthened or repaired without excavation?	The design will include an underpinning technique that minimises excavation and contact with contaminated material (e.g. mini-piles?). Identify contaminants by site investigation.	Highlight need to ventilate confined spaces inside building during work. Identify need to monitor confined spaces.

A GENERAL PLANNING

B 7 EXCAVATIONS AND FOUNDATIONS

C PRIMARY STRUCTURE

D BUILDING ELEMENTS AND BUILDING SERVICES

E CIVIL ENGINEERING

Related Issues

References within this document

References	Related issues
A1	Surrounding environment may be affected by the underpinning work.
A2	Site clearance may be moved before work can commence.
A3	Site investigation will be necessary to identify scope of work.
A4	Access onto the site will be a major consideration.
A5	Site layout may influence the underpinning method and temporary works.
B1	General excavation may be necessary.
B6	Piling may be used as a method of support.
C1,C2	Concrete pumping and use will need to be considered.
	Groundwater level and surcharge from plant will influence stability of trench excavations.
	Contaminated ground will influence design and precautions.
E3	Working near railways will be a major consideration in the choice of plant..
E6,E7	Working near water will involve possibility of dewatering excavation.

References for Further Guidance

Primary general references and background information given in Section 4

Primary

- CITB Construction Site Safety Note 10 - Excavations
- Thornburn & Hutchinson Underpinning (Surrey University Press)
- HSE CIS8 (revised) Safety in excavations
- CIRIA Report 97 Trenching practice 1992

Secondary

- BRE Digest 381 Site investigation of low rise buildings - trial pits

Background

- CIRIA Technical Note 95 Proprietary trench support systems 1986 (microfiche only)

Classification

CAWS Group D, **CEWS** Class C,F&P, **CI/SfB** Code (1-)B

Group C - Primary structure
1 - General concrete

C1

Read the Introduction (page 9) before using the following guidelines

Scope

- Construction/maintenance/demolition procedures.
- Consideration of working at height or depth.
- Size of any pour, construction joints, expansion joints, movement joints and their positions.
- Element size/length/weight.
- Ducts, holes, chases, cutting, drilling.
- Falsework, formwork, shuttering.
- Bearings/connections/movement joints, water bars.
- Surface preparation, grit blasting, chemical retarders, expanded metal.
- Prefabrication - advantage, reduction of different activities.

Exclusions

- Ornamental concrete.
- Gunite/shotcrete.
- Grout.

GENERAL PLANNING	A
EXCAVATIONS AND FOUNDATIONS	B
PRIMARY STRUCTURE	C 1
BUILDING ELEMENTS AND BUILDING SERVICES	D
CIVIL ENGINEERING	E

Major Hazards

Refer to the Introduction (page 9) for details of accident types and health risks

Falling from height
Operatives falling during: preparation of falsework, formwork, concreting, curing.

Health hazards
Cement dust.
Wet concrete:
- skin/eye irritation,
- caustic burning.

Noise
Concrete:
- compaction,
- scabbling,
- breaking.

Inhalation of dust
Concrete :
- demolition,
- drilling/cutting,
- scabbling.

Impact
Concrete vibrators.
Concrete pumps.
Moving plant contact.
Skips, dumpers.

Fumes/heat
Cutting/thermic lances:
- inhalation,
- burns.

Specific Hazard Identification

Possible key considerations:

- **Materials choice** - Show that concrete is the appropriate material.
- **Properties** - Can elements, properties, features be standardised to simplify working procedures?
- **Prefabrication** - Show off-site fabrication design has been maximised.
- **Procedure** - Show that material is being handled appropriately.
- **Materials** - When is the concrete deleterious to: skin, eyes, inhalation, ingestion?
- **Climate** - Show that effects will not be exacerbated by sun, wind, cold, heat or water.
- **Emissions** - Will the process cause: fire, fumes, spray, dust, toxins?
- **Protection** - Has the need for additional protection been identified: enclosure, extraction, isolation, personal protection?
- **Any others?**

Prompts

- Location
- At height/depth
- Materials properties
- Element size
- Prefabrication
- Construction joints
- Holes/services
- Cutting
- Fixings
- Weight
- Demolition
- Access

Hazards Consideration in Design

Stage	Considerations and issues	Possible design options to avoid or mitigate hazards identified for general concrete
Concept Design	<ul><li>Why use concrete?</li><li>Scope of use</li><li>Familiar? - materials - application - location</li><li>Environment</li><li>Materials</li><li>Demand on resources</li></ul>	<ul><li>Having chosen to use concrete, will it be identified where it will be mixed and placed? Can it be safely located in that position?</li><li>If in-situ concrete, does the site have sufficient space for batching or is ready - mixed concrete available, within reasonable access to the point of placing?</li><li>Is the way in which the material is to be used known to the proposed contractors?</li></ul>
Scheme Design	<ul><li>Technology known?</li><li>Characteristics</li><li>Complexity</li><li>Programme</li><li>Review</li><li>Process</li><li>Protection</li><li>In-situ concrete</li><li>Pre-cast concrete</li><li>Pre-stressed concrete</li></ul>	<ul><li>Are special concrete mixes being used and can they be supplied locally to the site?</li><li>Consider the programme: where and when will the concreting be carried out? - outside or undercover? - in summer or winter?</li><li>Will concreting be at ground level and units raised or lowered? or prepared and concreted at height or depth?</li></ul>
Detail Design	<ul><li>Elements</li><li>Standardisation</li><li>Features</li><li>Holes/fixing</li><li>Cutting</li><li>Constituents</li><li>Method</li><li>Plan/control</li><li>Testing</li><li>Monitoring</li><li>Analysing</li></ul>	<ul><li>If the design requires a specific method of build, set it down for the contractor.</li><li>A safe method of construction should be determined by the designer.</li><li>Optimise standard unit details to minimise errors.</li><li>Include details for relevant stages in the life of the concrete element, construction, use, maintenance and demolition, chases, fixings, conduits, etc.</li><li>Chases or holes should be detailed to be cast into the unit and not cut or drilled later.</li></ul>

Examples of Risk Mitigation (methods of solution)

ISSUE ACTION	Concrete frame building	Working at height to install embedded fixing in RC element
Avoidance Design to avoid identified hazards but beware of introducing others	Avoid working at height by fabricating elements off-site.	Fixing installed in element off-site to avoid working at height.
Reduction Design to reduce identified hazards but beware of increasing others	Element prefabricated (e.g. reinforcement). Fabricate at ground level and lift.	(Does not apply if risk can be avoided)
Control Design to provide acceptable safeguards for all remaining identified hazards	Provide information of element construction.	(Does not apply if risk can be avoided)

Examples of Risk Mitigation (issues addressed at different stages)

An existing bridge over a busy road is to be upgraded. The abutments are adequate but the concrete deck and beams need to be replaced. The major risk is working at height and restricted access.

Concept design	Scheme design	Detail design
Consider fabrication off-site to avoid site activities at height over the road.	The beams will be pre-cast concrete. Tee beams chosen to provide immediate access for operatives to the bridgedeck.	Pre-cast units to be designed with service ducts, street furniture fixings and temporary protection included, to avoid on-site activities.

Concrete chambers are required to facilitate maintenance inspection of underground services. The variable ground conditions and limited working space indicate that working at depth within the excavations is a major risk.

Concept design	Scheme design	Detail design
Hazard studies have indicated that inspection chambers should be reinforced concrete to reduce hazardous activities in excavations, at depth.	To reduce hazards of depths, the inspection chambers will be pre-cast on-site and lowered into position. The additional hazards introduced by this method have been considered preferable to those being avoided.	Inspection pit design will include cast-in ducts, step irons, fixings, lifting points.

GENERAL PLANNING — A

EXCAVATIONS AND FOUNDATIONS — B

PRIMARY STRUCTURE — C 1

BUILDING ELEMENTS AND BUILDING SERVICES — D

CIVIL ENGINEERING — E

C1 Group C - Primary structure
1 - General concrete

Related Issues

References within this document

References	Related issues
A1	Surrounding environment for precautions to control spread of concrete materials.
A2	Site clearance will need controls to prevent pollution from concrete dust.
A3	Site investigation may be required to determine the extent and condition of the concrete.
A4	Access onto the site will be carefully planned to transport concrete or the constituent materials.
A5	Site layout will need to be co-ordinated with the requirement for concreting facilities.
C2	Insitu concrete will need to consider this work sector.
C3	Precast concrete will consider this work sector.
C4	Prestressed concrete will consider this work sector.
D1	External cladding may be made of concrete.
D5	Surface coatings and finishes may be an application to concrete products.
D10	Vertical transportation needs to be carefully considered when transporting concrete.
E1	Civil engineering small works will most likely use concrete.
E2	Roads, working adjacent to, maintenance.
E3	Railways, working adjacent to, maintenance.
E4	Bridge construction will probably use concrete.
E5	Bridge maintenance will cover concrete elements.
E6	Working over/near water may place concrete in an aggressive environment.
E7	Cofferdams in water are likely to be concrete.

References for Further Guidance

Primary general references and background information given in Section 4

Primary

- CIRIA Report 146 Design and construction of joints in concrete structures 1995
- HSE HS(G)46 A guide for small contractors - Site safety and concrete construction
- HSE CIS26 (revised) Cement
- BS 5975: 1996 Code of practice for falsework

Secondary

- CIRIA Technical Note 138 Planning to reduce noise exposure in construction 1990
- CIRIA Report 67 Tables of minimum striking times for soffit and vertical formwork 1991
- CIRIA Report 136 Formwork striking times 1995
- CIRIA Special Publication 57 Handling of materials on site 1988
- HSE GS28 Parts 1 to 4 Safe erection of structures

Background

- CIRIA Special Publication 97 Environmental handbook for building and civil engineering projects - design and specification 1994
- CIRIA Report 120 A guide to reducing the exposure of construction workers to noise 1990

Classification

CAWS Group E, **CEWS** Class F,G,H, **CI/SfB** Code (2-)q

Group C - Primary structure
2 - In-situ concrete

C2

Read the Introduction (page 9) before using the following guidelines

Scope

- Falsework - scaffolding, patent structure, steelwork, timber.
- Formwork - temporary, permanent, erecting, striking, pour sizes, construction joints.
- Reinforcement - spacing, grouping, supporting, projecting.
- Positioning concrete - skips, pumps, barrows, shute, tremmie.
- Placing concrete - spreading, levelling, loading, finishing (power float/tamp etc.).
- Concrete compaction - vibrating poker, tamper, external vibrators.
- Striking formwork/falsework - concrete maturity.
- Temporary loading conditions - temporary design, temporary support.

Exclusions

- No-fines concrete.
- Dry-lean concrete.
- Demolition.

Major Hazards

Refer to the Introduction (page 9) for details of accident types and health risks

Falls from height
Accessing or working on scaffold, preparing for or placing in-situ concrete, access, working on formwork.

Noise, vibration
Working with vibrators scabblers, saws, etc.

Collapse
Formwork/falsework permanent structure collapse under loading from fresh concrete, excessive spans, large sections.

Moving Plant
Collision with moving machines (concrete trucks, concrete mixers, pumps, dumpers, etc.).

Health hazards
Inhalation of dust from cement, modifiers or scabbling concrete for surface preparation and blowing out pours.

Irritants
Concrete constituent materials, mould oils:
- skin/eye irritation
- caustic burns.

GENERAL PLANNING — A

EXCAVATIONS AND FOUNDATIONS — B

PRIMARY STRUCTURE — C 2

BUILDING ELEMENTS AND BUILDING SERVICES — D

CIVIL ENGINEERING — E

A GENERAL PLANNING

B EXCAVATIONS AND FOUNDATIONS

C 2 PRIMARY STRUCTURE

D BUILDING ELEMENTS AND BUILDING SERVICES

E CIVIL ENGINEERING

Specific Hazard Identification

Possible key considerations:

- **Conditions** - Where are all the temporary and permanent conditions listed?
- **Design** - How is it shown that the element is designed to satisfy all the temporary and permanent conditions?
- **Temporary works** - Demonstrate how hazards have been checked in falsework and formwork design.
- **Access** - Show adequate access for plant, materials and operatives has been identified.
- **Space** - Show there is adequate space for access and working.
- **Environment** - Demonstrate the working environment is satisfactory.
- **Work Access** - Where is access to work areas set out?
- **Storage** - Show that materials storage areas have been considered.
- **Prefabrication** - Show that prefabrication has been maximised.
- **Any others?**

Prompts

- Access
- Transporting materials
- Positioning materials
- Formwork/falsework
- Pour sizes
- Construction joints
- Reinforcement
- Concreting
- Compaction
- Protection
- Loading

Hazards Consideration in Design

Stage	Considerations and issues	Possible design options to avoid or mitigate hazards identified for insitu concrete
Concept Design	• Why in-situ concrete? • Scope of work • Overall mass • Familiar to use • Accessibility set out • Interfaces defined • Characteristics • Programme plan	• Can the in-situ concrete work be safely constructed in the time available or should alternatives be considered (e.g. pre-cast concrete)? • Does the in-situ concrete work constitute a significant part of the work? If the in-situ work is not extensive, avoid sophisticated details. • Avoid using in-situ concrete at height or depth if possible.
Scheme Design	• Temporary works • Review complexity • Span/section defined • Sequence planned • Temporary loading • Tolerances set out • Protection defined • Procedures set down • Falsework design • Formwork design	• Use a design that allows for adequate access to construct the element on site, given selected production methods. • Will the formwork for the site concreting be open and accessible, or restricted and congested? • If the design assumes a specific construction (and demolition) sequence of build, identify it clearly in the design. • Inform formwork/falsework designer of element design assumptions.
Detail Design	• Access planned • Formwork detail • Falsework detail • Reinforcement • Pour sequence • Pour sizes • Curing/maturity • Striking criteria • Testing materials	• Ensure that it is possible to have safe access and place of work to construct the element. • Reinforcement cages or mats should be rigid. Avoid congestion of reinforcement in an element. • Identify reasonable pour layouts/sizes, with only reinforcement lap lengths protruding from the pour. • If the design assumes a depropping/striking time criterion (strike before/not until), ensure that it is clearly identified for the contractor in the health and safety plan.

Group C - Primary structure
2 - In-situ concrete

GENERAL PLANNING — A

Examples of Risk Mitigation (methods of solution)

ACTION \ ISSUE	Site activities	Surface preparation
Avoidance Design to avoid identified hazards but beware of introducing others	Avoid working in confined areas.	Avoid scabbling by co-ordinating construction joints and reinforcement arrangement.
Reduction Design to reduce identified hazards but beware of increasing others	Simplify and standardise details.	Specify use of surface retarders for joint preparation.
Control Design to provide acceptable safeguards for all remaining identified hazards		

Examples of Risk Mitigation (issues addressed at different stages)

A framed building is to be constructed on a congested site. The frame is not a regular grid; spans and loading vary. One option is to design for a reinforced concrete frame founded on a continuous raft.

Concept design	Scheme design	Detail design
Concept reviews indicate that an in-situ concrete structure is the simplest form of construction for this irregular building, thus reducing hazards.	Design to standardise beam/slab column sizes wherever possible. Reinforcement details and construction joints planned to suit shutter assembly on site.	The specification requires the construction joint preparation to be carried out using a surface retarder to reduce noise and dust hazards from concrete surface preparation.

A reinforced concrete retaining wall is being built along the side of a road in a town centre as part of a road improvement scheme. Earlier considerations indicate that insitu concrete is the preferred option. The retaining wall has to be founded at depth in order to reach ground with sufficient bearing capacity. The design will need to take into consideration the difficult working conditions to be encountered on site in close proximity to a busy road.

Concept design	Scheme design	Detail design
The design will reduce the hazards on site by minimising and separating the number of activities required to be carried out at depth.	Reinforcement and formwork will be fabricated off-site, delivered in panels at the surface and lowered into position, to reduce activities at depth.	Control procedures will be required to monitor air quality in the excavation, which will be affected by traffic exhaust gases.

Sidebar tabs: GENERAL PLANNING A | EXCAVATIONS AND FOUNDATIONS B | PRIMARY STRUCTURE C 2 | BUILDING ELEMENTS AND BUILDING SERVICES D | CIVIL ENGINEERING E

A | GENERAL PLANNING
B | EXCAVATIONS AND FOUNDATIONS
C 2 | PRIMARY STRUCTURE
D | BUILDING ELEMENTS AND BUILDING SERVICES
E | CIVIL ENGINEERING

Related Issues

References within this document

References	Related issues
A1	Surrounding environment will need to be considered when examining access to the pour location.
A2	Site clearance and simple demolition may be relevant in order that in-situ concreting activities can proceed.
A3	Site investigation may have to be carried out before the criteria for the design of the reinforced concrete works can be established.
A4	Access on the site will need to be determined to ensure the safe construction of the in-situ concrete.
A5	Site layout intersects with decisions to use in-situ concrete.
B2	Deep basements shafts are likely to use in-situ concrete construction.
B4	Retaining walls are likely to use in-situ concrete construction.
B6	Piling should be considered, as bored piling will use in-situ concrete construction.
B7	Under-pinning works will use in-situ concrete construction.
C1	General concrete
C3	Pre-cast concrete may be considered as an alternative to in-situ reinforced concrete.
C4	Pre-stressed, post-tensioned concrete may be also considered as an alternative to reinforced concrete.
E1	Civil engineering, small works are likely to be using in-situ reinforced concrete structures.
E4	Bridge construction may well be constructed in in-situ reinforced concrete.
E5	Bridge maintenance will probably require periodic attention to in-situ concrete details.
E6	Working over/near water is likely to use in-situ concrete.
E7	Cofferdams in water may use in-situ concrete.

References for Further Guidance

Primary general references and background information given in Section 4

Primary

- HSE HS(G)46 A guide for small contractors - Site safety and concrete construction
- HSE HS(G)32 Safety in falsework for insitu beams and slabs
- HSE CIS 26 (revised) Cement
- BS5975:1996 Code of practice for falsework

Secondary

- HSE GS28 Parts 1 to 4 Safe erection of structures
- CIRIA Report 67 Tables of minimum striking times for soffit and vertical formwork 1991
- CIRIA Report 136 Formwork striking times 1995
- CIRIA Report 108 Concrete pressure on formwork 1985
- CIRIA Special Publication 57 Handling of materials on site 1988

Background

- CIRIA Special Publication 118 Steel reinforcement 1995

Classification

CAWS Group E, **CEWS** Class F, **CI/SfB** Code (2-)E

Read the Introduction (page 9) before using the following guidelines

Scope

- Pre-cast work on site - cast adjacent to final location.
- Pre-cast work offsite - resultant effect of pre-cast construction decisions on the site.
- Transportation - from off-site pre-cast yard to construction site.
- Lifting - during fabrication, transportation, installation.
- Positioning - setting out, tolerances, locating, securing.
- Bearings/supports - adequacy, stability, temporary works.
- Fixings and holes/openings for handrails, ladders, barriers, services, chases.
- Finishes - to avoid site preparatory activities.
- Temporary loading, supporting, propping, bracing.

Exclusions

- Railway works (see E3).
- Marine works.
- Pre-stressed concrete (see C4).
- Cladding panels (see D1).

Major Hazards

Refer to the Introduction (page 9) for details of accident types and health risks

Falling from height
Operatives falling while accessing, locating or fixing pre-cast units.

Crushing
Lifting procedure for unit not defined in design:
-     adequate lifting points
-     maturity of concrete at lifting.

Collapse:
Pre-cast unit unable to carry loading or insufficiently restrained in temporary condition.

Collapse
Units placed in wrong position (inverted or on their side or located with incorrect bearing).

Collapse:
Pre-cast composite units may fail if not propped to carry the in-situ topping and temporary load.

Handling
Pre-cast unit is a shape/weight that is difficult to transport, lift or position.

A GENERAL PLANNING

B EXCAVATIONS AND FOUNDATIONS

C 3 PRIMARY STRUCTURE

D BUILDING ELEMENTS AND BUILDING SERVICES

E CIVIL ENGINEERING

Specific Hazard Identification

Possible key considerations:

- **Tolerance control** - encourages rapid and safe assembly.
- **Work at height** - Where are critical considerations?
- **Temporary conditions** - Are the assumed temporary conditions set down? Show that it is designed for fabrication, lifting, transport placing, temporary loading, etc.
- **Installation** - Do the units require installation procedures that are not likely to be routine on site?
- **Procedures** - Ensure that the procedures described for unit installation are sufficiently comprehensive.
- **Insitu stitch** - Where are details of in-situ infills or topping?
- **Any others?**

Prompts

- Access/transport
- Mock-up
- Handling points
- Unit weights
- Lifting procedures
- Transporting
- Positioning
- Temporary support
- Composite action
- Orientation
- Demolition
- Training

Hazards Consideration in Design

Stage	Considerations and issues	Possible design options to avoid or mitigate hazards identified for pre-cast concrete
Concept Design	• Why pre-cast? • Scope of work • Familiarly used? • Define accessibility • Interfaces set out • Sequence defined • Overall mass • Technology known	• Do the pre-cast concrete elements form an insignificant part of the work? Are they to be cast on site? If so, try to ensure details are simple. • Clearly define the designers' intended construction sequence • Are the units large? Can they be easily transported and handled and positioned on site? • Can pre-cast units be easily and safely positioned in their likely location?
Scheme Design	• Pre-stressed? • Unit characteristics • Span/section known • Shape identified • Number of units • Loading condition • Protection defined • Tolerances set out • Procedures defined	• Is the pre-cast supplier likely to have made similar units previously? • Ensure that the limits of size, weight and number are known by all parties as soon as possible. • Specify how the units are to be protected, handled, lifted and positioned. Include lifting points. • Ideally the units should be lifted and finally located direct from their transporter.
Detail Design	• Handling designed • Handling formwork and reinforcement • Surface treatment • Cutting/sawing • Inserts/fixings • Positioning/locate • Temporary support	• Ensure that all holes, chases, conduits, fixings, etc. are cast into the precast unit. • Ensure that detailing of reinforcement cages provides for easy lifting. Identify lifting points. • Minimise and simplify locating and fixing procedures and details especially at height or depth.

Examples of Risk Mitigation (methods of solution)

	ISSUE	
ACTION	**Element design**	**Connections/tolerances**
Avoidance Design to avoid identified hazards but beware of introducing others	Standardise unit size and shape.	Simplify unit shape for tolerance control.
Reduction Design to reduce identified hazards but beware of increasing others	Consider limit for unit size/shape/weight.	Simplify lifting fixing/connection details.
Control Design to provide acceptable safeguards for all remaining identified hazards	Detail unit handling procedures/training.	Specify location/ connection procedures.

Examples of Risk Mitigation (issues addressed at different stages)

Apartment blocks on a site are required to be built within a short site construction period. To achieve the programme and budget, it has been decided to maximise the off-site fabrication process. One option is the use of pre-cast concrete for structural elements.

Concept design	Scheme design	Detail design
Pre-cast construction, judged to allow greater standardisation - avoids hazards of complicated in-situ details and work on site.	Standardise units where possible. Consider dimensions, weight and shape of units. Design for loads during lifting.	To reduce handling and fixing hazards, the pre-cast units will include cast-in connections for handling, positioning, hand rails and running lines

An office block is to be built over vaulted arches which are to be retained. The columns for the offices pass through the vaulting and are founded below the vaults. Due to lack of headroom in the vaults and high loading, the foundations are proposed to be hand-dug caissons with an option to use pre-cast segmental rings as liners.

Concept design	Scheme design	Detail design
This application of caissons is not a familiar technique. Designers are examining the pre-cast liner option in order to avoid hazards of collapse.	A design study determines that a 3 segment pre-cast concrete liner reduces hazards over the in-situ option.	Mock-up trials indicated pre-cast liner segments should include lifting sockets, grout/water seals, grouting and vent tubes and escape ladder fixings.

GENERAL PLANNING — A

EXCAVATIONS AND FOUNDATIONS — B

PRIMARY STRUCTURE — C 3

BUILDING ELEMENTS AND BUILDING SERVICES — D

CIVIL ENGINEERING — E

Related Issues

References within this document

References	Related issues
A1	Surrounding environment will need to be considered with regard to transporting and positioning pre-cast units.
A2	Site clearance may be required in order to prepare for access and positioning of pre-cast units.
A3	Site investigation could be required in order to finalise which elements are pre-cast.
A4	Access will be required for the transportation, positioning and placing (or removal) of the unit.
A5	Site layout will interact with access, positioning and placing of pre-cast units.
B1	General excavations could entail the use of pre-cast units. Ensure they will resist the conditions.
B2	Deep basements/shafts may use pre-cast units as lining in segmental form for retaining structures.
B3	Trenches for foundations and services, pre-cast units may be used to carry services.
B4	Retaining walls - may be pre-cast concrete.
B6	Piling - may use pre-cast concrete for driven piles.
C1	General concrete - ensure the pre-cast units perform adequately.
C2	In-situ concrete may be considered as an alternative for pre-cast concrete.
C4	Pre-stressed, post-tensioned concrete may be pre-cast concrete.
D1	External cladding likely to be pre-cast if it is to be made of concrete.
E1	Civil engineering, small works will frequently use pre-cast concrete units.
E4	Bridge construction may be entirely or partly pre-cast concrete.
E5	Bridge maintenance could entail the maintenance of pre-cast concrete units and the sealing, joints etc.
E6	Working or near water could use pre-cast concrete.

References for Further Guidance

Primary general references and background information given in Section 4

Primary

- CIRIA Technical Note 137 Selection and use of fixings in concrete and masonry 1991
- CIRIA Special Publication 57 Handling of materials on site 1988
- Precast Concrete Frameworks Association Code of practice for safe erection of pre-cast concrete frameworks

Secondary

- BS5975:1996 Code of practice for falsework
- CIRIA Technical Note 104 Pre-cast concrete tunnel linings 1981
- HSE GS28 Parts 1 to 4 Safe erection of structures

Background

- BS7121: Code of Practice for safe use of cranes
  - Part 1: 1989 General
  - Part 2: 1991 Inspection, testing and examination
- CIRIA Special Publication 131 Crane stability on site 1996

Classification

CAWS Group E, **CEWS** Class H, **CI/SfB** Code (2-)f

Read the Introduction (page 9) before using the following guidelines

Scope

- Post-tensioned reinforced concrete.
- Reinforcement - span, anchor zones, duct supports.
- Stressing ducts - gauge, profile, fixing, jointing.
- Stressing cables - wires, strands.
- Anchorage zones - anchor blocks, wedges, jacks.
- Grouting - grouting tubes, venting, duct profiles.
- Stressing procedure - when, sequence, linear, monitor, precautions.
- Materials - concrete maturity, strength, creep, shrinkage.
- Demolition.

Special Notes:

1. Stresses used in pre-stressed concrete are usually very high. Care must be taken in design and use of all materials

2. Wire = single

   Strand = multi-wire

   Tendon = multi strand

Exclusions

- Pre-stessed pre-tensioned concrete.
- Externally post-tensioned structures e.g. silos, bridges.
- Pre-stressed non-reinforcement concrete structures eg. ground anchors.

Major Hazards

Refer to the Introduction (page 9) for details of accident types and health risks

Falls from height
Operatives fall from access/ elements during fixing/ stressing.

Collapse/crushing
Units unstable in temporary condition (high d/b ratio).

Impact/collapse
Strand breakages during stressing:
- strand damage or duct obstruction/defect
- duct alignment.

Inadequate access
Operatives unable safely to access work area, poor materials handling facilities.

Collapse
Duct breaks loose and floats during concreting (duct support failure).

Impact/collapse
Collapse of element during demolition.
Inadequate support and failure of compression zone during demolition.

GENERAL PLANNING   A

EXCAVATIONS AND FOUNDATIONS   B

PRIMARY STRUCTURE   C 4

BUILDING ELEMENTS AND BUILDING SERVICES   D

CIVIL ENGINEERING   E

Group C - Primary structure
4 - Pre-stressed, post-tensioned concrete

A — GENERAL PLANNING

B — EXCAVATIONS AND FOUNDATIONS

C 4 — PRIMARY STRUCTURE

D — BUILDING ELEMENTS AND BUILDING SERVICES

E — CIVIL ENGINEERING

Specific Hazard Identification

Possible key considerations:

- **Assumptions** - Where are the design assumptions stated clearly?
- **Materials** - How will materials be maintained in good condition on site?
- **Access** - Show that the design will allow sufficient working space.
- **Design** - Show that the design avoids strand, anchor, reinforcement congestion.
- **Support** - Provide adequate support for stressing ducts.
- **Grouting** - Check grout vents are to be at highest point of duct profile.
- **Ducts** - How are stressing ducts kept clear of obstructions and water?
- **Strands** - Ensure strands are not snagged in ducts.
- **Any others?**

Prompts

- Protect materials
- Access for fixing
- Access for stressing
- Stressing protection
- Grouting procedure
- Handling points
- Transportation
- Demolition

Hazards Consideration in Design

Stage	Considerations and issues	Possible design options to avoid or mitigate hazards identified for pre-stressed concrete
Concept Design	• Why pre-stress? • Scope of work • Plan accessibility • Define interfaces • Sequence assumed • Overall mass • Technology known?	• Pre-stressing can be hazardous if inadequate design guidance to the contractor. • Loads and stresses are high - more easily controlled in a factory? Are the elements to be made on site? • Will the necessary construction expertise be locally available to the site?
Scheme Design	• Unit characteristics • Span section review • Number of units • Loading conditions • Locate tendons • Anchorage access • Duct support • Stressing protection • Tolerances defined • Procedures defined	• Units should be standardised wherever possible. • Prepare the design so that it allows the work to be carried out on site in good working conditions. • Ensure that the design sequence allows the contractor to provide good access. • Design and detail to reduce the risk that the materials will be damaged prior to or during installation (e.g. to reduce ad hoc repair work on site).
Detail Design	• Care of materials • Tendon layout • Duct profile, radii, joints, vents • Anchorage layout • Strands replaced • Stressing sequence • Grouting sequence • Striking supports • Deflection/creep • Loading application	• Specify conditions for materials storage, dry, well laid-out, clean, secure, etc. • Be aware of strand installation method when designing ducts. • Design duct supports. • Ensure adequate spacing for anchorages. • Avoid dead-end anchorages. • Specify installation procedures and controlled inspections of work. • Specify protection of materials, installation and completed work. • Detail control procedures prior to, during and after tendon stressing to reduce risk of hazards occurring.

Examples of Risk Mitigation (methods of solution)

ACTION	ISSUE	
	Reduce and simplify site activities	**Cable failure during post-tensioning**
Avoidance Design to avoid identified hazards but beware of introducing others	Pre-construct off-site or at ground level.	Avoid stressing duct congestion.
Reduction Design to reduce identified hazards but beware of increasing others	Pre-stressed proposals simplified and good access provided.	Smooth stressing duct profile.
Control Design to provide acceptable safeguards for all remaining identified hazards	Outline competence level required and highlight the need to co-ordinate with concurrent trades.	Outline stressing procedures.

Examples of Risk Mitigation (issues addressed at different stages)

A building constructed in the 1930s has undergone change of use to offices. This requires a review of the existing rivetted steel frame.

Concept design	Scheme design	Detail design
To carry additional loading, it requires long span plated steel beams to be upgraded. The beams will be cased in reinforced concrete and post-tensioned in order to carry the new floor loading.	The composite post-tensioned solution avoids hazards of gas cutting and welding, while minimising noise and dust	Provide relevant information to Planning Supervisor for sequence of working and design assumptions.

The ramp beams are to be built for an elevated road deck. Due to alignment, the elevated ramp structure is complex and the design needs to reduce the hazards of congested construction at height.

The geometry of the beams are complex due to curved alignment on plan and elevation. The beam depth will be restricted by headroom constraints below them.

Concept design	Scheme design	Detail design
The ramp beams for an elevated road deck are to be cast in-situ post-tensioned concrete, instead of pre-cast, in order to avoid difficult details of casting PC units, but will now involve increased work at height.	The in-situ design has avoided the hazards associated with complex layout of stressing tendons.	To reduce hazards, details provide adequate spacing of anchor blocks in relation to stressing jack requirements.

GENERAL PLANNING **A**

EXCAVATIONS AND FOUNDATIONS **B**

PRIMARY STRUCTURE **C 4**

BUILDING ELEMENTS AND BUILDING SERVICES **D**

CIVIL ENGINEERING **E**

Related Issues

References within this document

References	Related issues
A1	Surrounding environment may have to be considered for stressing procedures and protection.
A2	Site clearance and simple demolition will need to identify those elements that are post-tensioned.
A3	Site investigation may be required to determine the extent and details of pre-stressed concrete within a structure.
A4	Access on the site will need to consider location and access to pre-stressed units.
A5	Site layout will need to identify the positioning of pre-stressed units, to design access and protection.
B4	Retaining walls may be designed with the use of pre-stressed concrete, (pre-tensioned or post-tensioned).
B5	Ground stabilisation may be carried out with the use of ground anchors (in effect, a form of post-tensioned concrete).
C1	General concrete will identify the constituents of the concrete in the pre-stressed member.
C2	In-situ concrete - Post-tensioned unit is more likely to be cast in-situ (in position).
C3	Pre-cast concrete - The post-tensioned units may be pre-cast prior to final location.
D7-D10	Services - Extreme caution should be exercised if services require the formation of builders work openings in pre-stressed units. They should all be pre-formed prior to concreting. Never cut on site.
E1-E8	Civil engineering works - Pre-stressed concrete frequently occurs in civil engineering works.
E4	Bridge construction is often pre-stressed concrete.
E5	Bridge maintenance should always check pre-stressed members during condition surveys.
E6	Working over/near water may use pre-stressed concrete.

References for Further Guidance

Primary general references and background information given in Section 4

Primary

- HSE GS49 Pre-stressed concrete
- CIRIA Guide 1 A guide to the anchor blocks for post-tensioned pre-stressed concrete 1976
- CIRIA Special Publication 57 Handling of materials on site 1988

Secondary

- CIRIA Report 28 The connection of pre-cast concrete structural members 1971
- CIRIA Technical Note 129 Prestressed concrete beams - Controlled demolition and pre-stress loss assessment 1987
- HSE HS(G) 46 A guide for small contractors - Site safety and concrete construction
- HSE GS5 Entry into confined spaces

Background

- BS5975: 1992 Code of practice for falsework

Classification

CAWS Group E,   **CEWS** Class H,   **CI/SfB** Code (2-)E

Read the Introduction (page 9) before using the following guidelines

Scope

- Building frames such as offices, schools, hotels, etc.
- Portal frames for agricultural or industrial premises.
- Towers and chimneys, assembled on site.
- Footbridges and other load carrying spans.
- Gantries for street signs/lighting and other similar.
- Atria or other facades based on a structural steel frame.
- Hot-rolled and cold-formed sections.

Exclusions

- Temporary works.
- Stability during erection (see C6).
- Corrosion/fire protection (see D5).
- Stressed skin designs.
- Cable tied and fabric structures.

Major Hazards

Refer to the Introduction (page 9) for details of accident types and health risks

Falls from Height
Placing, stability and provision of working platforms, access.

Collapse
Storage areas, stacking and stability, falling objects, access, temporary bracing.

Hazardous operations
Cutting/Welding.
Painting.
Descaling.

Mobile Plant
Delivery, traffic control, offloading, slinging.
Site routes.

Moving objects
Remedial works, plumbing, levelling.
Trapping.
Manual handling.

Noise, vibration
Bolting, drilling.
Reaming.

Sidebar tabs:
- A — GENERAL PLANNING
- B — EXCAVATIONS AND FOUNDATIONS
- C 5 — PRIMARY STRUCTURE
- D — BUILDING ELEMENTS AND BUILDING SERVICES
- E — CIVIL ENGINEERING

C5 Group C - Primary structure
5 - General steelwork

Specific Hazard Identification

Possible key considerations:

- **Delivery** - How will pieces be manoeuvred to and onto site?
- **Logistics** - How will delivery match sequence of use?
- **Lifting** - What are the requirements to allow the (tower) crane driver the facility to lift and position the pieces safely?
- **Storage** - Where and how will items be stored as they are unloaded?
- **Stability** - When unloaded, how will stability of the pieces be controlled?
- **Access** - How will hand and power tools be used at the work site?
- **Working at height** - How will working at height be accomplished?
- **Light and air** - What sorts of local environments are involved?
- **Other activities** - How could the works affect other people? How might the workforce be affected by what is going on around them?
- **Any others?**

Prompts

- Lifting
- Access
- Transport
- Positioning
- Alignment and fit-up
- Reaming
- Slotted holes
- Connection type
- Corrosion protection
- Welding
- Cutting
- Bolting
- Painting

Hazards Consideration in Design

Stage	Considerations and issues	Possible design options to avoid or mitigate hazards identified for general steelwork
Concept Design	• Why use steelwork? • Scope of work • Element sizes • Piece weights • Manoeuvrability • Equipment • Site Environment	• Exploit the facility to quickly erect and achieve stability; a safe working platform offers specific safety advantages. • Determine how the steel frame can provide working platforms for subsequent work and other trades. • Assess methods for delivery, storage, pre-assembly and erection of steelwork to safeguard construction workers. • Metal decking for composite slabs offers significant safety advantages during construction (e.g. stabilises the structure, provides safe working platform).
Scheme Design	• Programme • Craneage • Working area • Sub assemblies • Movement joints • Temporary loads • Interface connections • Sequencing of work • Connection types	• Show how structure might be built to anticipate and eliminate (if possible) hazards. • Consider how temporary/erection loads can be accommodated without the need for additional members or framing. • Explore how pre-assembly off and on site can enhance health and safety. • Consider installing staircases earlier to provide safer access. • Ensure adequate bracing is provided as the frame is erected
Detail Design	• Bolt types • Temporary conditions • Pre-assembly • Lining and levelling • Tolerances • Painting • Testing	• Consider advantages of repetition (e.g. one size, fully-threaded bolts) to reduce complexity of hazardous work. • Ensure that connections are dimensionally tolerant to avoid need for remedial works at height. • De-burr holes and grind arrises to make components safer to handle. • Eliminate/reduce need for work on site at height by ensuring an adequate base is prepared to allow safe working of mechanical lifting plant. • Avoid complex connections.

Group C - Primary structure
5 - General steelwork

Examples of Risk Mitigation (methods of solution)

ACTION \ ISSUE	Moving and storing materials	Working at height
Avoidance Design to avoid identified hazards but beware of introducing others	Place steelwork straight from the lorry	Consider pre-assembly on the ground
Reduction Design to reduce identified hazards but beware of increasing others	Establish site to provide adequate laydown areas away from site traffic	Design-in lifting points and/or methods to release crane hooks remotely.
Control Design to provide acceptable safeguards for all remaining identified hazards	Use guys and timbers to support steelwork until placed in position	Incorporate safety harness attachment points in detailing

Examples of Risk Mitigation (issues addressed at different stages)

For a large portal frame warehouse, the designer wants to provide access within the building envelope for other works while the steel frame is being erected and before the building is clad and finally braced.

Concept design	Scheme design	Detail design
A sequence of construction is designed so that other trades can rapidly follow on behind steelwork erection; bracing provided so that structural stability always maintained.	A method of pre-assembly and erection is established to ensure that the contractor can be advised of a way in which it can be built safely.	Baseplates and foundation are detailed to provide adequate resistance to overturning, by using four bolts to accommodate temporary conditions.

A building refurbishment project involves the retention of a listed facade and the reconstruction of part of the building to link up to a 1930s steel-framed structure.

Concept design	Scheme design	Detail design
Member serial sizes and lengths are kept down to a size which can be "threaded" into the structure without requiring a tower crane.	Bolted connections are adopted throughout because of the problem of welding in confined spaces with a lot of adjacent activity.	Connections are designed to be dimensionally tolerant, so that risk of misfit is minimised.

A — GENERAL PLANNING

B — EXCAVATIONS AND FOUNDATIONS

C 5 — PRIMARY STRUCTURE

D — BUILDING ELEMENTS AND BUILDING SERVICES

E — CIVIL ENGINEERING

C5 — Group C - Primary structure
5 - General steelwork

Sidebar tabs:
A GENERAL PLANNING
B EXCAVATIONS AND FOUNDATIONS
C5 PRIMARY STRUCTURE
D BUILDING ELEMENTS AND BUILDING SERVICES
E CIVIL ENGINEERING

Related Issues

References within this document

References	Related issues
A1	Surrounding environment will need to be considered when examining access to deliver steelwork.
A2	Site clearance and simple demolition may be needed so that steelwork storage and placing activities can proceed.
A4	Access on the site will need to be determined to ensure the safe construction.
A5	Site layout may interact with the decision to use steelwork, particularly if pre-assembly is used more generally.
C1	General concrete is usually used for foundations for steelwork.
C6	Temporary stability is a dominant issue when considering safe design in steelwork.
D3	Atria are invariably designed in steelwork with glazing infill.
D5	Surface coatings and finishes will always be required on exposed steelwork.
D10	Lifts and travelators could have steel framing or have steelwork linking it to a concrete core.
E4	Bridge construction may be steel and always has health and safety considerations.
E5	Bridge maintenance will probably require periodic attention to steelwork.
E6	Working over/near water may use any steelwork.
E7	Cofferdams in water may use steelwork.

References for Further Guidance

Primary general references and background information given in Section 4

Primary

- HSE GS 28 Parts 1 to 4 Safe erection of structures
  Part 1 Initial planning and design
  Part 2 Site management and procedures
  Part 3 Working places and access
  Part 4 Legislation and training
- CIRIA Special Publication 131 Crane stability on site 1996
- CIRIA Special Publication 57 Handling of materials on site 1988

Secondary

- British Constructional Steelwork Association - Structural Steelwork Fabrication
- Steel Construction Institute - Steel Designer's Manual
- CIRIA Report 87 Lack of fit in steel structures 1981

Background

- BS 7121: Code of Practice for safe use of cranes
  Part 1: 1989 General
  Part 2: 1991 Inspection, testing and examination

Classification

CAWS Group G, **CEWS** Class M, **CI/SfB** Code (28)h2

Read the Introduction (page 9) before using the following guidelines

Scope

- Site pre-assembly.
- Pre or part erection.
- Temporary works.
- Interim connections.
- Erection stability.
- Plumbing and levelling.
- Temporary bracing.
- Structural cores.
- Interfaces with other trades.
- Connections.

Exclusions

- Temporary storage or laydown.
- Launched structures.
- Stressed skin designs.
- Cable tied and fabric structures.
- Demolition.

Major Hazards

Refer to the Introduction (page 9) for details of accident types and health risks

Falls from height
Placing, stability and provision of working platforms, access.

Collapse
Excessive loading or load reversal.
Inadequate ties, struts or bracing.
Incorrect sequence.
Incomplete assembly.

Noise vibration
Pneumatic and manual wrenches and hammers.

Harmful Substances
Sparks and heat from burning and welding.
Electricity
Paints, greases etc.

Moving objects/trappings
Placing of steelwork. Closure of joints.
Sharp objects.
Baseplate packing.

Refer also to Sector C5 hazards

A GENERAL PLANNING

B EXCAVATIONS AND FOUNDATIONS

C 6 PRIMARY STRUCTURE

D BUILDING ELEMENTS AND BUILDING SERVICES

E CIVIL ENGINEERING

Specific Hazard Identification

Possible key considerations:

- **Handling** - How are units to be brought together/ assembled?
- **Assembly** - What different methods of assembly are safest for this site?
- **Buildability** - Determine at an early stage how the structure might be built safely. Repeatedly reconsider this as design proceeds to ensure that safety is maintained or enhanced.
- **Structural Capacity** - Which methods and sequences of assembly could inadvertently lead to overloading?
- **Stability Core** - If any parts of the structure rely upon other particular parts for their stability, is this obvious?
- **Site Condition** - What site conditions could affect these works? How can these be designed out?
- **Pieces (and bundles) of steel** could have their weight marked and locations and orientations shown, making placement easier.
- **Manoeuvring** - Once on the crane hook, do loads need additional control? How will this be provided?
- **Any others?**

Prompts

- Local access
- Visibility
- Ground stability
- Surrounding environment
- Confined spaces
- Temporary guys/struts
- Alignment
- Special connections
- Corrosion protection
- Welding
- Cutting
- Loose fit pieces
- Cleaning and painting
- Checking and testing
- Base grouting

Hazards Consideration in Design

Stage	Considerations and issues	Possible design options to avoid or mitigate hazards identified for stability and erection of structural steelwork
Concept Design	• Scope of work • Form of construction • Building shape/size • Pre-assembly • Sequences • Major Plant	• Because the highest incidence of accident and injuries arise from "falls from height" this must be a special consideration when considering ways to allow safe work on partially-erected steel frames. • Consider sequence of site/structure development to determine the most appropriate option.
Scheme Design	• Site access • Craneage • Ground conditions • Work sequences • Sub-assemblies • Element sizes/weights • Temporary loads • Work platforms • Inter-connections	• Can the steel frame erection be conceived as inherently stable sub-assemblies? • Consider if welding, HSFG, or bolts in bearing offer any particular health and safety benefits - e.g. by providing temporary moment capacity. • Assess structure to see if areas can be rapidly developed to act as stable work platforms. • Design so that stairways can be installed ahead of frame erection, for safer access.
Detail Design	• Connection details • Lot sizes and sequences • Column bases • Temporary storage • Bolt types and sizes • Tightening and torquing • Tolerances	• For ease of erection, seek to use fewer - or even one - size of bolt throughout. • Can elements in tension also be designed to accept temporary compression loads (to provide enhanced stability)? • Ensure that structural mechanism assumed for method of construction is communicated to all who might need to know. • Include temporary working platforms and/or harness attachment points.

Examples of Risk Mitigation (methods of solution)

ACTION / ISSUE	Assembly stability	Making connections
Avoidance Design to avoid identified hazards but beware of introducing others	Design for assembly at ground level and to have fewer but larger lifts. Ensure provision of base for cranage.	Adopt positive seating systems. Explore range of connection types.
Reduction Design to reduce identified hazards but beware of increasing others	Outline sequence of construction which allows in-built stability.	Specify one size, fully-threaded free running bolts to simplify work at height.
Control Design to provide acceptable safeguards for all remaining identified hazards	Outline temporary support.	Allow for use of hydraulic platform for jointing at height.

Examples of Risk Mitigation (issues addressed at different stages)

Because the top three storeys of a building cantilever out over other structures, the engineer has arranged that they structurally "hang" from a central core in the final condition. During erection, however, the steel frame can be sufficiently light as to be temporarily supported from the outrigger areas of the floors below.

Concept design	Scheme design	Detail design
Establish work platform/crash deck areas and deal with tower crane oversailing to ensure practicality	Identify construction sequence to allow structure to develop on a floor-by-floor basis.	Design "hangers" also for temporary role as columns, to ensure stability at all stages of erection.

A steel footbridge is to be erected over a busy highway which serves a housing estate, a school and a shopping precinct.

Concept design	Scheme design	Detail design
A single span is chosen, to minimise working adjacent to traffic and to reduce dangers to road vehicles.	A lightweight design is adopted so that it can be lifted into place during a single weekend night-time road closure. Minimum temporary works required for temporary stability.	Connections and lifting points in the steelwork are designed to allow rapid pre-assembly adjacent to the site.

GENERAL PLANNING **A**

EXCAVATIONS AND FOUNDATIONS **B**

PRIMARY STRUCTURE **C 6**

BUILDING ELEMENTS AND BUILDING SERVICES **D**

CIVIL ENGINEERING **E**

Related Issues

References within this document

References	Related issues
A1	Surrounding environment will need to be considered when examining access to site.
A2	Site clearance and simple demolition may be relevant for steel erection.
A3	Site investigation may have to be carried out before design of the column bases.
A4	Access on the site will need to be determined to ensure safe construction .
A5	Site layout may affect the decisions to use steelwork.
C1	General concrete.
C5	General steelwork.
D3	Atria - Invariably have temporary and final stability issues to be resolved.
D5	Surface coatings and finishes - will always be part of erecting steelwork.
D10	Vertical transportation - often a part of the stability core of a structure.
E4	Bridge construction may well be constructed using steel.
E5	Bridge maintenance will probably require periodic attention to steelwork details.
E6	Working over/near water will be likely to use steelwork.
E7	Cofferdams in water may use steel.

References for Further Guidance

Primary general references and background information given in Section 4

Primary

- BS 5531: 1988 Code of practice for safety in erecting structural frames
- HSE GS28 Parts 1 to 4 Safe erection of structures
- CIRIA Special Report 131 Crane stability on site 1996

Secondary

- British Constructional Steelwork Association - Structural Steelwork Erection
- Steel Construction Institute - Steel Designer's Manual
- CIRIA Special Publication 57 Handling of materials on site 1988

Background

- BS 7121: Code of Practice for safe use of cranes
  Part 1: 1989 General
  Part 2: 1991 Inspection, testing and examination

Classification

CAWS Group G, **CEWS** Class M, **CI/SfB**, Code (28)h2

Group C - Primary structure
7 - Masonry

Read the Introduction (page 9) before using the following guidelines

Scope

- Brickwork.
- Blockwork.
- Stonework.
- Pre-assembled composite masonry/brickwork units.
- Jointing materials.
- Positioning of pre-assembled elements including setting out, locating and securing.
- Bearings/supports of pre-assembled elements.
- Temporary loading and supporting.
- Reinforcement in masonry work.

Exclusions

- Masonry cladding (see D1).
- Gabions/crib block walls.
- Post-tensioned masonry.

Major Hazards

Refer to the Introduction (page 9) for details of accident types and health risks

Handling
Weight, shape, transportation of units. Working space, hoists, manual handling at height.

Hazardous substances
Cement handling, lime and mortar mixing, chemical grouts, additives, dust.

Access
Delivery/offloading. Plant on site. Obstruction by other building elements. Working space restrictions.

Crushing
Placement of units, insufficient space for storage/working, falling objects, vehicle movements.

Collapse
Unpropped construction, elements being overloaded, movement joints, storage/stacking irregular units, horizontal chases, DPC debonding.

Abrasion/cuts
Masonry texture, wall ties, metal lathing, sheet metal Insulation (glass fibre).

A — GENERAL PLANNING

B — EXCAVATIONS AND FOUNDATIONS

C 7 — PRIMARY STRUCTURE

D — BUILDING ELEMENTS AND BUILDING SERVICES

E — CIVIL ENGINEERING

Specific Hazard Identification

Possible key considerations:

- **Handling** - How will the units be handled? Manually or by crane?
- **Access** - What provisions are required to ensure adequate space for plant and scaffolding?
- **Temporary conditions** - What design considerations are involved?
- **Installation** - How can this be arranged to ensure healthy and safe procedures?
- **Special considerations** - What are the required procedures (e.g. cutting)?
- **Jointing materials** - What are these to be? How will they be applied?
- **Masonry ties** - What can be specified to make installation safer?
- **Any others?**

Prompts

- Source of materials
- Handling units
- Handling points
- Lifting procedures
- Transporting units
- Positioning
- Temporary support
- Lime and other chemicals
- Cleaning
- Demolition

Hazards Consideration in Design

Stage	Considerations and issues	Possible design options to avoid or mitigate hazards identified for masonry
Concept Design	• Why use masonry? • Location • Scope of work • Familiar work • Access • Interfaces • Sequences • Materials	• The alternatives to using masonry will generally involve in-situ or pre-cast concrete. If not, design masonry that has familiar details. • Can stone work be factory prepared? In particular, can site cutting of sandstone be avoided? • Plan the timescale and sequence of masonry working to avoid working during bad weather, during winter months or on a congested site. • Study alternative routes for access. Allow adequate working space for operatives and materials.
Scheme Design	• Unit types • Joints • Handling • Reinforcement • Protection • Tolerances • Procedures • Working space • Handling	• Specify materials that are least likely to create dust (e.g. use preformed materials). • Avoid blocks above 20kg weight. • Consider components that are preformed and joined on site. • Consider methods of quick and secure erection. • Joint design tolerances should be relevant to nature of work. • Design provision for delivery and handling of materials on congested sites, close to work station if possible.
Detail Design	• Inserts/fixings • Connections/joints • Finishes • Bearings • Positioning • Temporary supports	• Wherever possible use materials that are non-corrosive and non-abrasive. • Specify appropriate tolerances to avoid cutting, etc. on site. • If mechanical handling is necessary, incorporate lifting and handling attachment points into the design. • Design-in provision for service runs, to avoid cutting on site.

Group C - Primary structure
7 - Masonry

Examples of Risk Mitigation (methods of solution)

ACTION	ISSUE Handling large blocks	Use of brickwork ties
Avoidance Design to avoid identified hazards but beware of introducing others	Use blocks less than 20kg, to allow manual handling.	Specify ties without sharp edges.
Reduction Design to reduce identified hazards but beware of increasing others	Detail lifting points for block handling.	Construct second skin as soon as possible.
Control Design to provide acceptable safeguards for all remaining identified hazards	Specify mechanical handling for laying large blocks.	Specify temporary covers to sharp ties (if used).

Examples of Risk Mitigation (issues addressed at different stages)

A refurbishment project requires selected stonework to be removed and replaced at height from a building due to weathering and moisture ingress. The new stonework is to match the existing.

Concept design	Scheme design	Detail design
Consider alternative safe methods for how the suspect stonework could be removed and replaced.	Develop a safe method of removal and replacement using scaffolding as access and also means of handling stonework.	To avoid hazards of cutting on site, special replacement stonework will be surveyed and prepared off-site.

Internal fair-faced walls to an exhibition centre are 8 metres high and are required to have the special effect of textured large concrete blocks with decorative joints.

Concept design	Scheme design	Detail design
Design for 2 leafs of blockwork, using 20kg blocks to reduce weight for manual handling.	Design 20kg blocks to incorporate provisions for the decorative joints.	Blockwork lifts not to exceed 1.5m high each day. Wall-ties selected to avoid hazards of handling and being cut by sharp edges. Highlight that care is required when using retarders.

GENERAL PLANNING — A
EXCAVATIONS AND FOUNDATIONS — B
PRIMARY STRUCTURE — C7
BUILDING ELEMENTS AND BUILDING SERVICES — D
CIVIL ENGINEERING — E

A GENERAL PLANNING

B EXCAVATIONS AND FOUNDATIONS

C 7 PRIMARY STRUCTURE

D BUILDING ELEMENTS AND BUILDING SERVICES

E CIVIL ENGINEERING

Related Issues

References within this document

References	Related issues
A2	Site clearance and simple demolition will involve the safe storage and removal of brickwork and general masonry.
A4	Access onto site will need to accommodate the frequent deliveries of materials for masonry work.
A5	Site layout will need to consider the safe storage of materials delivered to site for masonry work.
B1-B3	Excavations are frequently for masonry work within deep excavations. Alternative methods should be considered (e.g. use of pre-cast rings).
B7	Underpinning to foundations could involve masonry work.
C1-C4	Concrete works usually interface with masonry works, with different trades working closely.
D1	External cladding often incorporates masonry panels.
E1	Civil Engineering small works may involve the use of engineering brickwork/masonry work, in difficult and remote locations.

References for Further Guidance

Primary general references and background information given in Section 4

Primary

- BRE Good Building Guide Repairing and replacing lintels
- HSE CIS 36 Silica
- HSE CIS37 Handling building blocks
- CIRIA Guide 4 Selection and use of fixings in concrete and masonry
- CIRIA Report 117 Replacement ties in cavity walls : a guide to tie spacing and selection 1988
- CIRIA Special Publication 57 Handling of materials on site 1988

Secondary

- BRE Good Building Guide 14 Building brick or blockwork freestanding wall positioning and ties
- BRE Defect action sheet 115 External masonry cavity wall, wall ties, selection and specification

Background

- BS56528: Code of practice for use of masonry
  Part 1: 1992, Structural use of unreinforced masonry
  Part 2: 1995, Structural use of reinforced and pre-stressed masonry
  Part 3: 1985, Materials and components, design and workmanship

Classification

CAWS Group F, **CEWS** Class U, **CI/SfB** Code (2-)F

Read the Introduction (page 9) before using the following guidelines

Scope

- Softwoods.
- Hardwoods.
- Wood-based products (e.g. plywood, chipboard).
- Glued laminated timber (Glulam).
- Building frames.
- Roof trusses (including "gang nail" trusses).
- Trussed partitions.
- Suspended floors.
- Preservative treatments.

Exclusions

- Repair of decayed timber.
- Fire protection of timber (cladding).
- Temporary works (falsework, shuttering, etc.).
- Support to suspect buildings.
- Surface painting.

Major Hazards

Refer to the Introduction (page 9) for details of accident types and health risks

Falls from height
Erection sequences during installation, edge protection, platforms, access.

Collapse
Temporary stability. Inadequate staging/support.
Ground support for cranes.
Stacked materials.

Health hazards
Wood preservatives.
Adhesives, resins.
Treated timber.
Wood dust.

Access
Site layout, delivery routes
Storage, cranage, erection sequences.

Mobile plant
Delivery lorries, site transport, cranes, dumpers, inadequate working space, erection sequences.

Handling
Off-loading, stacking and erecting components (manual and use of crane). Metal connectors/cleafs.
Cuts and splinters.

Sidebar:
GENERAL PLANNING — A
EXCAVATIONS AND FOUNDATIONS — B
PRIMARY STRUCTURE — C 8
BUILDING ELEMENTS AND BUILDING SERVICES — D
CIVIL ENGINEERING — E

C8 — Group C - Primary structure
8 - Timber

Sidebar tabs:
A — GENERAL PLANNING
B — EXCAVATIONS AND FOUNDATIONS
C 8 — PRIMARY STRUCTURE
D — BUILDING ELEMENTS AND BUILDING SERVICES
E — CIVIL ENGINEERING

Specific Hazard Identification

Possible key considerations:

- **Assumptions** - What are the design assumptions? Do they imply health or safety hazards?
- **Handling and storage** - How will the components be off-loaded and stored?
- **Sequences** - What are the construction sequences?
- **Access** - How will adequate access and working space be maintained?
- **Weather** - What are the likely weather conditions?
- **Installation** - What procedures are necessary for unit installation?
- **Temporary support** - What provisions will be necessary?
- **Fire walls** - What is construction against fire walls?
- **Any others?**

Prompts

- Temporary conditions
- Transport
- Access
- Lifting points
- Positioning, alignment
- Connections
- Tolerances
- Preservatives
- Adhesives
- Demolition

Hazards Consideration in Design

Stage	Considerations and issues	Possible design options to avoid or mitigate hazards identified for timber
Concept Design	• Why use timber? • Scope of work • Interfaces • Site environment • Programme • Outline sequences	• The alternatives to timber will usually include steel or concrete. • Fire prevention is a major consideration when using timber. • Study the options for access and working space, in conjunction with construction sequences available within the constraints of the site. • Examine the feasibility of just-in-time delivery of pre-fabricated units.
Scheme Design	• Major equipment • Access • Component sizes and weights • Working space • Storage areas • Handling methods • Installation • Pre-assembly • Cranage	• Review component sizes and weights together with handling methods. • Develop arrangements for just-in-time delivery, to enable direct placement of the unit into the final position. • Identify handling methods to suit methods of supply and storage. • Examine sequences of construction, to avoid unnecessary overlapping of activities and other trades.
Detail Design	• Temporary supports • Preservatives • Tolerances • Connections • Lifting points • Positioning	• If mechanical handling is necessary, incorporate lifting and handling measures into the design. • Devise permanent works to incorporate temporary support. • Develop joint arrangements which minimise cutting on site. • Specify preservatives that are not hazardous to operatives during application; preferably apply preservatives in factory conditions.

Examples of Risk Mitigation (methods of solution)

	ISSUE
ACTION	**Roof erection**
Avoidance Design to avoid identified hazards but beware of introducing others	Design for pre-fabricated roof at ground level, place by crane.
Reduction Design to reduce identified hazards but beware of increasing others	Lift trusses by crane and provide space for use of hydraulic platforms.
Control Design to provide acceptable safeguards for all remaining identified hazards	Incorporate handling points and positive seating.

Examples of Risk Mitigation (issues addressed at different stages)

A leisure facility is to include a large enclosed space. The architect wishes to incorporate a timber finish to the main structural members. Site investigation results indicates that a lightweight structure is required to provide acceptable bearing pressures.

Concept design	Scheme design	Detail design
Structural members are to be designed using glued-laminated timber columns and timber roof trusses. Use of timber means lower capacity cranes for erection. These can be used working within the building on a prepared granular base.	Specify allowable tolerances and temporary wind bracing requirements to ensure stability during erection. Lightweight tiles to be used.	Design pre-fabricated crane-handled hips and valley sets to minimise working at height.

A timber structure is to be constructed against an existing Grade 1 Listed Building. Due to the unconformity of the building, significant site cutting and jointing is envisaged. The cut surfaces will need to be treated with preservatives.

Concept design	Scheme design	Detail design
Design members to maximise pre-fabrication and minimise make-up pieces and site application of preservatives.	Specify application requirements for preservative treatment. Maximum in pre-fabrication works by vacuum pressure treatment. Design make-up pieces.	Design site connections to make application of preservatives easily accessible and minimise working at height.

Group C - Primary structure
8 - Timber

Related Issues

References within this document

References	Related issues
A1	Surrounding environment will need to be considered when examining access to the installation locations.
A2	Site clearance and simple demolition may be relevant in providing adequate access and storage areas.
A3	Site investigation will usually need to be carried out to determine criteria for the design of the timber structure.
A4	Access onto site and adjacent to installation location will need to be considered to ensure safe construction.
A5	Site layout may interact with decision to use timber construction.
D2	Roofs are likely to be constructed using timber trusses.
E6	Working over/near water may be an important consideration when working on timber construction.

References for Further Guidance

Primary general references and background information given in Section 4

Primary

- TRADA Timber in construction
- CIRIA Report 111 Structural renovation of traditional buildings (updated 1994)
- CIRIA Special Publication 57 Handling of materials on site 1988

Secondary

- Baird and Ozlatan, Timber Designer's Manual
- The Trussed Rafter Manual - Gangnail systems
- BS5268: Part 5: 1989 Code of practice for preservative treatment of structural timber

Background

- BS5268: Part 3: 1985 Code of practice for trussed rafter roofs
- BS4169: 1988, Specification for manufacture of glued-laminated structural members

Classification

CAWS Group G,   **CEWS** Class O,   **CI/SfB** Code (2-)i

Group D - Building elements and building services
1 - External cladding

Read the Introduction (page 9) before using the following guidelines

Scope

- Factory fabricated panel cladding systems.
- Site assembled traditional frame systems.
- Panel rainscreen cladding systems.
- Panel overcladding systems.
- Thin stone and brick veneers.
- Profiled metal sheeting including composite panels.

Exclusions

- Brickwork/blockwork (see C7).
- Insulated and non-insulated renders.
- Special glass assemblies (e.g. Pilkington's Planar Glazing)
- Special finishes (e.g. patination).
- Restoration.

Major Hazards

Refer to the Introduction (page 9) for details of accident types and health risks

Working at height
Workers falling during erection, cleaning, maintenance and repair. Dropped objects during erection, maintenance and repair.

Replacement
Access, size of pieces to be moved round building and into position, ease of removal, safe fixing.

Glazing
Accidental breakage, site glazing, replacement glazing from outside, large pieces of glass, annealed glass.

Handling/transportation
Many stages - on/off lorries, in/out of storage, up/down building, into final position on building, repair/maintenance.

Hazardous operations
Surveys prior to installation. Glazing, testing, site welding, cutting, maintenance.

Hazardous substance
Paints, sealants, insulating materials.

GENERAL PLANNING — A

EXCAVATIONS AND FOUNDATIONS

PRIMARY STRUCTURE — C

BUILDING ELEMENTS AND BUILDING SERVICES — D1

CIVIL ENGINEERING — E

A GENERAL PLANNING

B EXCAVATIONS AND FOUNDATIONS

C PRIMARY STRUCTURE

D1 BUILDING ELEMENTS AND BUILDING SERVICES

E CIVIL ENGINEERING

Specific Hazard Identification

Possible key considerations:

- **Building location** - Are there particular access problems? Do the public have to be protected? Will the site exclude using particular plant, cladding system or materials?

  Building form - Can the cladding be prefabricated? Can large panels be installed and fixed safely to all elevations? Are there any difficult to construct features (e.g. overhangs)?

- **Repair and maintenance** - What suitable methods and equipment for cleaning, inspection and maintenance? Will this equipment allow replacement of pieces of cladding (e.g. glass)?

- **Life of cladding** - Will some or all elements of the cladding need replacement? Can replacement be carried out safely? Can the cladding be dismantled safely?

Prompts

- Materials (heavy/light)
- Size of pieces (man lift or machine)
- Life to first maintenance and failure maintenance
- Glaze from inside or out
- Replacement
- Fixings (easy to install)
- Access to site
- Access round the building
- Adjustment/alignment/tolerances
- Any restricted spaces
- Jointing/sealing
- Cleaning
- Large and lightweight panels
- Wind loading effect

Hazards Consideration in Design

Stage	Considerations and issues	Possible design options to avoid or mitigate hazards identified for external cladding
Concept Design		• Study forms of cladding construction that allow safe working space for operatives and safe lining and levelling once on the building. • Check whether planning/budgetary/client restraints permit the use of permanently installed facade cleaning and maintenance equipment. • Identify variations to the building shape which suit cladding that can be constructed, cleaned and maintained safely.
Scheme Design	• Location • Building shape • Form of construction • Access for plant/people • Cleaning, repair and maintenance • Sequence of operations • Method of assembly • Element size/weight • Interfaces • Temporary conditions • Connections/fixings • Adjustment/alignment • Testing	• Develop cladding details to provide primary attachments that are safe and easy to use in all locations. • Develop cladding jointing details that permit safe and easy installation. • Design elements so that they can be cleaned and replaced safely.
Detail Design		• If mechanical handling is required, incorporate lifting and handling measures into the design. • If restraints are required for cleaning and maintenance equipment incorporate these into the design. • Co-ordinate with designer of structural frame to ensure primary fixings are safe and easy to install.

Examples of Risk Mitigation (methods of solution)

ACTION / ISSUE	Falls during cleaning	Hazardous operation fixings
Avoidance Design to avoid identified hazards but beware of introducing others	Provide permanently installed access equipment that can be entered without stepping over a building edge.	Provide primary attachments to the frame that slot together without the need for loose bolts.
Reduction Design to reduce identified hazards but beware of increasing others	Provide suitable access round the building to allow lorry-mounted access platforms to reach all parts of the facade.	Provide primary attachments to the frame that allow bolts to be placed without the need to work overhead.
Control Design to provide acceptable safeguards for all remaining identified hazards	Provide a comprehensive system of attachments and latchway wires for personal protective equipment.	Provide a greater number of primary attachments to the frame so that smaller bolts can be used.

Examples of Risk Mitigation (issues addressed at different stages)

An existing office building in the centre of a major city is to be refurbished and reclad. The building is bounded on two sides by existing buildings and on the other two sides by very busy city streets and public pavements. There is no room for a crane or a large hoist, and the internal goods lift is small.

Concept design	Scheme design	Detail design
Large prefabricated panels cannot be lifted. A traditional aluminium framing system is appropriate with infill elements designed to fit the lifting arrangements and access round the building.	The sequence of operations is planned so that the elements needed to complete sections of wall are delivered to site in crates of a size to suit the lifting arrangements and access round the building.	Design the primary attachments so that they can be safely installed from the inside at each floor level.

The project involves the overcladding of a seven-storey block of local authority flats. The block is brick-clad, concrete framed, with timber-framed single-glazed windows. The local authority wants to change the municipal appearance, improve thermal performance and reduce maintenance costs without moving the occupants.

Concept design	Scheme design	Detail design
A metal rainscreen overcladding system with insulation behind meets the brief. The issues associated with fixing insulation and the problems of noise/dust/isolation when installing fixings need to be considered.	A cleaning and maintenance strategy is developed to allow windows to be cleaned from inside and the main facade from roof mounted access equipment.	A sequence of operation is developed for removing existing windows and filling new ones into the overcladding system without too much disruptions to the occupiers.

Related Issues

References within this document

References	Related issues
D6	Cleaning and maintenance is fundamental to cladding design and must be considered at the earliest possible time.
A4	Access onto and around the site may dictate the cladding that has to be used.
C1-C8	Primary structure will dictate the type of fixing and the amount of adjustment required to take up tolerances safely.
	Interfaces for different trades will dictate sequencing of operations and replacement and maintenance strategies.
	Operators should be aware that maintenance and repair companies are sometimes less knowledgeable than the original installers/designers. Keep maintenance and repair to a minimum by good design and the use of appropriate materials.
	Occupied buildings, maintain safe access/egress and fire escape if the building is occupied while work is in progress.

References for Further Guidance

Primary general references and background information given in Section 4

Primary

- CIRIA Special Publication 57 Handling of materials on site 1988
- Glass and Glazing Federation - Working with Glass
- BS 6262: 1982 Code of practice for glazing for buildings
- BS 6037: 1990 Code of practice for permanently installed suspended
- BS 8213: 1991 Part 1 Code of practice for safety in use and during cleaning of windows and doors

Secondary

- Standing Committee on Structural Safety (SCOSS)
  Report No. 8 (1989) - Section 3.7 Cladding failures
  Report No. 9 (1992) - Section 3.7 Cladding and Controls over cladding repair and refurbishment
  Report No. 10 (1994) - Section 3.3 Special structures, components and materials, sub-sections cladding and glazing
- HSE CIS 5 (revised) Temporarily suspended access cradles and platforms
- CIRIA Book 5 Rainscreen cladding, a guide to design principles and practice, 1988

Background

- BS 6206: 1981 (1994) Specification for impact performance requirements for flat safety glass and safety plastics for use in buildings
- BS 2830: 1994 Specification for suspended access equipment for use in the building, engineering, construction, steeplejack and cleaning industries
- BS 5974: 1990 Code of practice for temporarily installed suspended scaffolds and access equipment
- HSE PM30 Suspended access equipment

Classification

CAWS Group H, **CEWS** Class Z, **CI/SfB** Code (41)

Group D - Building elements and building services
2 - Roof coverings and finishes

Read the Introduction (page 9) before using the following guidelines

Scope

- Flat roofs.
- Pitched roofs.
- Terraces and balconies.
- Car park/service decks.
- Skylights and rooflights.

Exclusions

- Fabric and membrane roofs (tents).
- Temporary protection roofs.
- Mansard roofs.
- Prefabricated domes, etc.

Major Hazards

Refer to the Introduction (page 9) for details of accident types and health risks

Falls from heights
Working at heights on steep pitches and slippery surfaces. Fragile roofs/rooflights. Lack of edge protection.

Access
Maintenance of roof and plant. Permanent or occasional use by building occupants, contractor (e.g. fire escape).

Hazardous materials and Hazardous operations:
Hot asphalt and bitumen, solvents and volatiles. Welding and soldering of metalwork.

Collapse
Temporary support structure, construction platform and permanent works.

Handling
Transport and handling of materials to and across the roof. Hazards from weight, size, temperature or chemical nature of materials.

Falling or dropping
Onto people below roof level. Items falling from unprotected roof perimeter or fragile zones within roof area (e.g. rooflights).

A — GENERAL PLANNING

B — EXCAVATIONS AND FOUNDATIONS

C — PRIMARY STRUCTURE

D2 — BUILDING ELEMENTS AND BUILDING SERVICES

E — CIVIL ENGINEERING

Specific Hazard Identification

Possible key considerations:

- What are the benefits of pitched versus flat roofs?
- What provisions and assumptions are made for temporary stability and safety?
- What provision is made for the effects of wind during construction and maintenance?
- Is the roof construction designed to minimise risks from exposure to chemicals (solvents/fumes) and hot materials?
- What are the weather conditions likely to be during installation?
- What are the fire risks?
- What people access is proposed for roof maintenance?
- Are there general or localised weak zones in the accessible roof area (eg. rooflights)?
- Can permanent edge protection/protected walkways be incorporated?
- Size and weight vs handling and wind resistance.

Prompts

- Stability and support
- Access
- Transport of materials
- Solvents and volatiles
- Hot working
- Rainwater disposal
- Windspeed and exposure
- Falling/dropping
- Design life
- Maintenance
- Edge protection
- Panel/roll size
- Fragility of materials
- Flashings (lead)

Hazards Consideration in Design

Stage	Considerations and issues	Possible design options to avoid or mitigate hazards identified for roof coverings and finishes
Concept Design		• A flat roof can provide a more secure work platform and access for maintenance. • A pitched roof can have a longer design life and require less maintenance.
Scheme Design	• Flat versus pitched • Building structure influence on roof type and covering. • Wind/rain exposure • Sequence of construction activities • Access to site and roof • Stability and support • Selection of roof system • Maintenance access • Lead flashing	• Security of roof components during construction and service will be affected by wind speed. • Particular wind phenomena occur at near roof perimeters and ridge. • The sequencing of roof construction will influence the risks of falling, temporary instability, weather hazards and problems of temporary storage on the roof. • Consideration needs to be given to the stability and support of each stage - temporary or permanent - of the roof construction; allow for possible loads at both stages.
Detail Design		• Selection of materials, handling and fixing to minimise hazards from installation. • When the design options will determine a sequence of working, favour the option/sequence which minimises the risks from temporary instability, lack of support, inclement weather working, difficult local access - partial covering of work by other traders. • Detail design to avoid wind uplift/water overload.

Examples of Risk Mitigation (methods of solution)

ACTION \ ISSUE	Falls during cleaning	Translucent fragile panels
Avoidance Design to avoid identified hazards but beware of introducing others	Loose lay cold membranes to avoid the use of hot bitumen.	Use alternative stronger material.
Reduction Design to reduce identified hazards but beware of increasing others	Use torch-applied bonding or solvents/adhesives to secure pre-formed products.	Use a thicker material or additional layers of material.
Control Design to provide acceptable safeguards for all remaining identified hazards	Specify maximum pour size.	Provide a walkway/grille over the fragile panels.

Examples of Risk Mitigation (issues addressed at different stages)

A large factory requires fast construction to bring the facility on stream. It is preferred that the roof be finished early in the programme so that other construction and fitting out can take place beneath in protected conditions.

Concept design	Scheme design	Detail design
Cost, programme considerations and repetitive nature of construction lead to choice of flat roof which can quickly follow frame erection. Rapid placement of metal decking not only provides safer work platform for use at height but also protects remainder of workforce at ground level from dropped objects and inclement weather.	Roofing materials to be mechanically fixed to minimise time spent at height and complexity/hazards of these work activities.	Final detailing of gutters/eaves to incorporate provision for edge protection primarily for construction, but which can also be exploited during maintenance.

Design of a pitched roofed warehouse with valley gutters.
The "traditional" roof appearance is preferred because of existing architecture and technical concerns.

Concept design	Scheme design	Detail design
Consider choice of roofing sheets. Reject fragile material as roof access is required for cleaning gutters.	Appropriate non-fragile material selected.	Make valley gutter wide enough and strong enough to walk along. Provide permanent edge protection at gable ends of gutters.

GENERAL PLANNING — A

EXCAVATIONS AND FOUNDATIONS — B

PRIMARY STRUCTURE — C

BUILDING ELEMENTS AND BUILDING SERVICES — D2

CIVIL ENGINEERING — E

Related Issues

References within this document

References	Related issues
A1	Surrounding environment will need to be assessed for access routes for materials and prevailing wind conditions.
A4	Access onto and within the site will need to be considered.
A5	Site layout could be influenced by roof construction type and associated methods.
C1-C8	Primary structure can influence roof construction options.
C8	Timber will often be used for trusses supporting roof coverings.
D1	External cladding details and roofs interact.
D4	Windows/glazing may be included in roofs and will require cleaning.
D7	Mechanical plant for services often have to be roof-mounted.
D8	Lightning protection.

References for Further Guidance

Primary general references and background information given in Section 4

Primary

- CITB - Construction site safety, Section 24 Safe working on roofs and at height
- BEC Construction Safety, Section 15 Work on roofs

Secondary

- BS6229: 1982 Code of practice for flat roofs with continuously supported coverings
- BS 5534: 1990 Code of practice for slating and tiling, Part 1
- HSE CIS 5 (revised) Temporarily suspended access cradles and platforms
- HSC - Approved Code of Practice - Control of lead at work

Background

- Copper in Roofing Pocket Book
- BS CP3: 1972 Chapter V: Wind loads, Part 2
- BS 6399: Part 2: 1995 Code of practice for wind loads
- CIRIA & BFRC Book 15 Flat Roofing guide: Design and good practice 1993
- BRE Digest 346: Assessment of Wind loads

Classification

CAWS Group H, **CEWS** Class W, **CI/SfB** Code (47)

Read the Introduction (page 9) before using the following guidelines

Scope

- Walls to atria.
- Roofs to atria.
- Roofs to shopping malls.

Exclusions

- Internal partitions.
- Rooflights and skylights.

Major Hazards

Refer to the Introduction (page 9) for details of accident types and health risks

Working at height
Falling from height,cleaning, maintenance and repair, access. Dropped objects.

Hazardous materials
Paints, sealants, glass.

Handling
Many stages on/off lorries, in/out of storage, up/down building into final position on building, repair maintenance.

Glazing
Site glazing, glazing from outside, large pieces of glass, replacement, accidental breakage, metal/glass contact.

Hazardous operations
Inspections, glazing and reglazing, cleaning and maintenance, servicing smoke vents.

GENERAL PLANNING — A

EXCAVATIONS AND FOUNDATIONS — B

PRIMARY STRUCTURE — C

BUILDING ELEMENTS AND BUILDING SERVICES — D 3

CIVIL ENGINEERING — E

Specific Hazard Identification

Possible key considerations:

- **Installation** - Has access for installation been considered? Do the public have to be protected? Will scaffolding be required? How are elements to be lifted? Fixed?

- **Cleaning and maintenance** - Consideration to be given to cleaning inside and outside. How is access for cleaning and maintenance to be achieved? Consider how replacement is carried out. Will other services interfere with cleaning?

- **Injury from falling objects** - Consider the use of safe materials overhead (e.g. laminated glass)? Can features be designed to protect people below from falling objects? Consider the use of handrails and other barriers to stop people and objects striking glass.

Prompts

- Access
- Maintenance
- Replacement
- People overhead
- Handling
- Occupied premises
- Tolerances
- Fixings (easy to reach)
- Jointing and sealing
- Other services
- Confined spaces

Hazards Consideration in Design

Stage	Considerations and issues	Possible design options to avoid or mitigate hazards identified for atria
Concept Design	• Access • Cleaning and maintenance • Form of construction • Shape and size • Design life	• Consider using purpose-designed permanently installed access equipment inside and outside overhead glazing for cleaning, maintenance and glass replacement. • Ensure safe access can be provided for installation • Ensure access to cleaning and maintenance equipment provided can be achieved safely.
Scheme Design	• Element size/weight • Sequence • Cranage • Repair replacement • Types of glass and configuration • Connections/fixings • Assembly • Temporary conditions during erection	• The design of the glazing system and associated cleaning equipment should maximise factory prefabrication. • Any external temporary scaffolding roofs required for construction should be designed to allow smoke extraction in the event of a fire.
Detail Design	• Adjustment/ • Alignment • Surveys of supporting structure • Testing of cleaning equipment • Sequence of assembly	• Fixing details for overhead glazing need to be detailed so that they can be secured without working overhead and blind. • Glazing systems need to be designed so that glass can be replaced without danger of whole sheets falling onto operatives.

Examples of Risk Mitigation (methods of solution)

ACTION	**ISSUE**	
	Falls during maintenance	**Injury from falling objects**
Avoidance Design to avoid identified hazards but beware of introducing others	Provide permanently-installed access equipment inside and outside the roofs to atria that can be entered without stepping over a building edge or onto the roof.	Use materials that will not fall out of supporting framework if they are broken accidentally.
Reduction Design to reduce identified hazards but beware of increasing others	Consider a strategy for maintenance that involves the regular erection of purpose designed scaffolding with access platforms at appropriate levels to allow safe working methods to be used.	Provide features below that will catch falling objects and direct them to areas where they will do no harm.
Control Design to provide acceptable safeguards for all remaining identified hazards	Provide a comprehensive system of attachments and latchway wires for personal protective equipment, with safe access onto these systems.	Prevent or limit access to the vulnerable elements by barriers or protection.

Examples of Risk Mitigation (issues addressed at different stages)

A glass roof over an atrium has suffered from spontaneous fracture of toughened glass panes due to nickel sulphide inclusions. The owner wishes to re-glaze the roof while the building is still in use. The base of the atrium is 5 storeys below the roof and is used as a circulation area.

Concept design	Scheme design	Detail design
A scaffolding will be erected with a working deck just below the roof. Temporary roofing will go over the glass roof.	Consider options for supporting the working deck/crash deck and temporary smoke control.	Identify risks associated with the assumed sequence and method of dismantling.

A new shopping centre is to be constructed. The mall between the shops is to have a glazed roof.

Concept design	Scheme design	Detail design
Consider various forms for the glazed roof that will allow for cleaning and maintenance. Assess options for access to building and maintenance equipment	Consider various types of cleaning equipment that can be used and select the one that offers the easiest and safest access for installation and maintenance.	Design safe and unobstructed access for maintenance cleaning equipment.

Side tabs: GENERAL PLANNING **A** / EXCAVATIONS AND FOUNDATIONS **B** / PRIMARY STRUCTURE **C** / BUILDING ELEMENTS AND BUILDING SERVICES **D 3** / CIVIL ENGINEERING **E**

A GENERAL PLANNING

B EXCAVATIONS AND FOUNDATIONS

C PRIMARY STRUCTURE

D3 BUILDING ELEMENTS AND BUILDING SERVICES

E CIVIL ENGINEERING

Related Issues

References within this document

References	Related issues
A4	Access onto the site and access for installing and cleaning atria cladding will dictate the form of cladding to be used and the sequence and method of assembly.
C1-C8	Primary structure will dictate the types and method of fixing and the amount of adjustment required to take up tolerances.
D6	Cleaning and maintenance is fundamental to atria design and must be considered at the earliest possible time.
	Interfaces for different trades will dictate sequencing of operations and replacement and maintenance strategies.
	Operators should be aware that maintenance and repair companies are sometimes less knowledgeable than the original installers/designers. Hence minimise maintenance and repair in design and use appropriate materials.
	Occupied building, maintain safe access/egress and fire escape if the building is occupied while construction cleaning or maintenance work is in progress.

References for Further Guidance

Primary general references and background information given in Section 4

Primary

- Glass and Glazing Federation - Working with Glass
- BS 5516: 1991 Code of practice for design and installation of sloping and vertical patent glazing
- CIRIA Special Publication 87 Wall technology Volumes B to G, 1992

Secondary

- Standing Committee on Structural Safety (SCOSS)
  Report No. 8 - Section 3.7 Cladding failures
  Report No. 9 - Section 3.7 Cladding & Controls over cladding repair and refurbishment
  Report No. 10 - Section 3.3 Special structures, components and materials, sub-sections cladding and glazing
- BS 6037: 1990 Code of practice for permanently installed suspended access equipment.

Background

- CIRIA Special Publication 57 Handling of materials on site 1988
- HSE CIS 5 (revised) Temporarily suspended access cradles and platforms
- HSE PM 30 Suspended access equipment

Classification

CAWS Group H, **CEWS** Class Z, **CI/SfB** Code (--) 913

Read the Introduction (page 9) before using the following guidelines

Scope

- New windows.
- Replacement windows.
- Windows in curtain walling.
- Windows in overcladding.
- Windows in brickwork/blockwork/stonework.
- Domestic windows.

Exclusions

- Rooflights/skylights (see D2).
- Special loading conditions (e.g. bomb blast).
- Smoke ventilators.

Major Hazards

Refer to the Introduction (page 9) for details of accident types and health risks

Working at height
Falling from height, cleaning, maintenance and repair, access, dropped objects.

Cleaning and maintenance
Outside of window difficult/dangerous to reach, rarely provision for access and working place.

Replacement
Access through occupied spaces and lack of protection outside.

Handling transportation
Many stages, on/off lorries, in/out of storage, up/down building, into final position on building.

Hazardous operations
Surveys prior to installation, glazing, testing cleaning and maintenance.

Hazardous materials
Paints, sealants, insulating materials, glass.

A GENERAL PLANNING

B EXCAVATIONS AND FOUNDATIONS

C PRIMARY STRUCTURE

D 4 BUILDING ELEMENTS AND BUILDING SERVICES

E CIVIL ENGINEERING

Specific Hazard Identification

Possible key considerations:

- **Installation** - Has access for installation been considered? Will the site exclude using particular plant or equipment? How are windows lifted? How are they fixed? Can the pieces be easily handled, moved and installed?

- **Cleaning and maintenance** - How is access for cleaning and maintenance achieved? How is replacement carried out? How will windows be opened for cleaning? Will size of opening light limit cleaning and maintenance options? Will permanently installed equipment be provided for the outside of the building.

- **Occupied buildings** - will the windows be installed, cleaned and maintained from inside the building? Will special tools or procedures be required to remove windows or glass in the event of failure? Access and escape routes need to be maintained at all times. Reduce hazardous operations to a minimum. Will other services interfere with installation, cleaning and maintenance?

Prompts

- Space to align local access
- Low cills
- Safe reach to outside
- Replacement
- Building in use
- Low maintenance materials
- Glaze from inside
- Adjustment/alignment
- Size of glass pieces

Hazards Consideration in Design

Stage	Considerations and issues	Possible design options to avoid or mitigate hazards identified for windows
Concept Design		• Consider options for cleaning maintenance and repair which include permanent or temporary access equipment. • To reduce maintenance requirements consider low maintenance options like coated aluminium or UPVC rather than timber. • Consider types of window to assist with cleaning and maintenance, e.g. centre pivot or reversible.
Scheme Design	• Building shape/size • Location • Cleaning strategy • Repair/maintenance • Form of construction • Opening type • Size of opening light • Temporary conditions • Connections fixings • Types of glass • Limiting stays • Opening devices • Locking devices • Sequence of assembly • Fixing details • Glazing details	• Replacement strategy will dictate the size of glass and window framing that can be moved through an occupied building. • Design of fixing should consider ease of adjustment for building tolerances and easy access from inside for replacement.
Detail Design		• Detail stays, restraints or guard rails to prevent window cleaners from falling out. • Detail components so that each element can be fixed and weathered without blind or overhead working.

Group D - Building elements and building services
4 - Windows/glazing including window cleaning

D4

Examples of Risk Mitigation (methods of solution)

ISSUE

ACTION

Falls during cleaning

ACTION	Falls during cleaning
Avoidance Design to avoid identified hazards but beware of introducing others	Clean externally from permanently installed access equipment that can be entered without stepping over a building edge, and limit size of windows so that they can be cleaned internally standing on the floor.
Reduction Design to reduce identified hazards but beware of increasing others	Provide centre pivot or reversible windows of limited size so that both sides can be cleaned safely from inside the building standing on the floor.
Control Design to provide acceptable safeguards for all remaining identified hazards	Provide inward opening windows of limited size and with locking stays so that both sides can be cleaned safely from inside the building standing on the floor and provide guard rails to protect the opening while the window is open.

Examples of Risk Mitigation (issues addressed at different stages)

A high rise office block by the sea is to have new windows fitted. Complaints about the air-conditioning from the users require the new windows to provide natural ventilation. The building will remain occupied during the work, though there will be a phased decanting of floors to allow the recladding work to proceed.

Concept design	Scheme design	Detail design
Consider whether reversible inward opening or pivot windows in the sizes required can be safely opened for cleaning in a windy environment. Can windows of the required size be installed from inside the building or does a strategy for installation, maintenance and replacement from outside have to be developed.	Consider the various types of the window selected and develop sequences of operations for installation and replacement that offer the easiest and safest means of access and egress.	Specify a window type that allows only narrow opening in everyday use, but wider opening with a special key for cleaning.

An extension of an existing building requires windows to match existing Georgian sash windows, but for acoustic reasons need to be triple glazed. The stone facade will not be cleaned regularly, the windows need to be cleaned regularly.

Concept design	Scheme design	Detail design
Establish a sequence of opening procedures that allows all faces of each piece of glazing to be reached from inside the building.	Confirm that the inward opening elements do not trap the cleaner or cause him to be pushed out of the window.	Detail the operating handles and safety catches to match the required sequence of opening and cleaning.

A — GENERAL PLANNING

B — EXCAVATIONS AND FOUNDATIONS

C — PRIMARY STRUCTURE

D 4 — BUILDING ELEMENTS AND BUILDING SERVICES

E — CIVIL ENGINEERING

Related Issues

References within this document

References	Related issues
A4	Access - Access onto the site and access for installing and cleaning windows will dictate the type of window used, and the sequence and method of installation.
C1-C8	Primary structure - the structure surrounding the windows will dictate the type and method of fixing and the amount of adjustment required to take up tolerances safely.
D6	Cleaning and maintenance - the strategy for cleaning and maintenance is fundamental to window design and must be considered at the earliest possible time.
	Interfaces - interfacing trades will dictate sequencing of operations and replacement and maintenance strategies.
	Operators - be aware that maintenance and repair companies are sometimes less knowledgable than the original installers/designers - so keep maintenance and repair to a minimum by good design and the use of appropriate materials.
	Occupied buildings - maintain safe access/egress and fire escape if the building is occupied while construction cleaning, maintenance or repair work is in progress.

References for Further Guidance

Primary general references and background information given in Section 4

Primary

- Glass and Glazing Federation - Working with Glass
- BS 8213: Part 1: 1991 Code of practice for safety in use and during cleaning of windows and doors
- BS 6262: 1982 Code of practice for glazing for buildings

Secondary

- Standing Committee on Structural Safety (SCOSS)
  Report No. 8 - Section 3.7 Cladding failures
  Report No. 9 - Section 3.7 Cladding and controls over cladding repair and refurbishment
  Report No. 10 - Section 3.3 Special structures, components and materials, sub-sections cladding and glazing
- BS 2830: 1994 Specification for suspended access equipment
- BS 5974: 1990 Code of practice for temporarily installed suspended scaffolds and access equipment
- BS 6037: 1990 Code of practice for permanently installed suspended access equipment
- HSE CIS 5 (revised) Temporarily suspended access cradles and platforms
- HSE PM30 Suspended access equipment.

Background

- BS 6206: 1981 (1994) Specification for impact performance requirements for flat safety glass and safety plastics for use in buildings

Classification

CAWS Group L, **CEWS** Class Z, **CI/SfB** Code (31.4)

Group D - Building elements and building services
5 - Surface coatings and finishings

Read the Introduction (page 9) before using the following guidelines

Scope

- Decorative coatings (paints) for timber, steel, concrete, plaster, masonry.
- Plaster, render and screeds.
- Corrosion and fire protection coatings (dry and wet systems).
- Floor and wall tiling.

Exclusions

- Composite sheet or board linings and cladding.

Major Hazards

Refer to the Introduction (page 9) for details of accident types and health risks

Toxic solvents
Solvents/volatiles from treatments or cleaning materials released into work space. Toxicity/suffocation if insufficient ventilation.

Fire
Combustibility and surface fire spread (including smoke).

Access and workplatform
Safety during application and maintenance.

Hazardous substances
Manmade mineral fibres, solvents, dust (silica).

Manual handling
Transport, storage and mixing of bulky/heavy materials.

Health
Noise, fume, dust. Resins and glues.

A **GENERAL PLANNING**

B **EXCAVATIONS AND FOUNDATIONS**

C **PRIMARY STRUCTURE**

D 5 **BUILDING ELEMENTS AND BUILDING SERVICES**

E **CIVIL ENGINEERING**

Specific Hazard Identification

Possible key considerations:

- **Handling and storage** - How will materials be off-loaded and stored?
- **Mixing** - What, if any, are the requirements?
- **Application method** - What are the options and implications?
- **Surface pre-treatment** - What operations are required?
- **Application** - What access to place of work is needed?
- **Weather conditions** - What are the application limitations?
- **Maintenance** - What are the requirements?
- **Materials** - What is the chemical nature?
- **Fire** - Is there a risk during application?
- **Any others?**

Prompts

- Solvents
- Transport
- Mixing
- Dust/fumes
- Maintenance
- Application equipment
- Access/place of work
- Working at height

Hazards Consideration in Design

Stage	Considerations and issues	Possible design options to avoid or mitigate hazards identified for surface coatings and finishings
Concept Design		• Can the same, or sufficient performance be achieved for the substrate without an applied finish (e.g. for light reflectance, or corrosion allowance)? • To what extent does the nature of the specific material selected, and its requirements for application either reduce hazards or generate new ones? • Sequence of construction consideration can identify situations where unacceptable hazards might occur (e.g. confined spaces and solvent release, working in unacceptable weather). • Do materials or components in contact require special pretreatment which might introduce a hazard (e.g. chemical interaction or relative movements)?
Scheme Design	• Why apply a finish? • Why spray apply finish? • Outline sequences • Compatibility of materials • Working space • Working environment • Ventilation • Pre-treatment • Handling • Access • Materials selection • Working sequence • Check existing surfaces	• Is sufficient space allowed for the operations and maintenance? • Is the working environment likely to be safe from hazards (e.g. toxic/suffocating fume release)? • Can pre-treatment be avoided without loss of performance?
Detail Design		• Choose pre-blended/pre-mixed materials to reduce handling. • Select solvent-less or water-based products wherever possible. • Study routes for access and handling materials and components. • Can materials be brought safely to the point of application? • Can the working sequence be modified to allow for better access or control of working environment?

Examples of Risk Mitigation (methods of solution)

ACTION \ ISSUE	Combustibility/fire spread	Access for application
Avoidance Design to avoid identified hazards but beware of introducing others	Use non-combustible products.	Factory preparation of substrate and application of coatings and finishes to avoid site work.
Reduction Design to reduce identified hazards but beware of increasing others	Use product of limited combustibility.	Only final layer/top coat or touching up to be site applied.
Control Design to provide acceptable safeguards for all remaining identified hazards	Limit application to low risk areas.	Access to height to be controlled by principal contractor.

Examples of Risk Mitigation (issues addressed at different stages)

A commercial office development wishes to offer prestige accommodation at an economic price. Space within the building for "non-productive" areas is under close scrutiny.

Plant rooms are only accessible by maintenance staff.

Concept design	Scheme design	Detail design
Plan space for optimum balance of plant requirements and maintenance of plant and surface finishes.	Provide access routes from outside building. Design adequate space for safe access to and maintenance of items of plants in plant rooms as well as access to walls, floors, etc. for maintenance of finishes.	If walls/floor need painting, select coatings which require little surface preparation, are water-based and/or solvent free and require low maintenance.

An existing warehouse is to be upgraded. The proposed works include fire - rating the steel frame.

Concept design	Scheme design	Detail design
Consider whether "dry" materials (board linings) can be used instead of "wet" materials (intumescent paint).	Consider the space available for the works and consider a method that minimises the hazards.	If "wet", specify pre-blended/mixed materials to reduce handling on site. Select solvent-free or water-based products wherever possible. If "dry", specify factory-cut boards.

GENERAL PLANNING — A

EXCAVATIONS AND FOUNDATIONS — B

PRIMARY STRUCTURE — C

BUILDING ELEMENTS AND BUILDING SERVICES — D 5

CIVIL ENGINEERING — E

Related Issues

References within this document

References	Related issues
A4	Access onto site will need to accommodate frequent deliveries of materials.
A5	Site layout will need to be considered for the delivery of materials to the point of application, and the safe storage of materials.
C2	In-situ concrete often has particular finishes specified.
C5	Structural Steelwork is often site painted.
C8	Timber treatments on site need to be planned with great care.

References for Further Guidance

Primary general references and background information given in Section 4

Primary

- HSE CIS 24 Chemical cleaners
- HSE CIS 27 Solvents
- BS 5492: 1990 Code of practice for internal plastering
- BS 5493: 1977 Code of practice for protective coating of iron and steel structures against corrosion
- BS 5262: 1991 Code of practice for external renderings
- BS 6150: 1991 Code of practice for painting of buildings
- BS 8000 Part 10: 1995 Workmanship on building sites: Code of practice for plastering and rendering
- BS 8000 Part 12: 1989 Workmanship on building sites: Code of practice for decorative wall coverings and painting

Secondary

- BS 8202: Part 1 (1995), Part 2 (1992) Coatings for fire protection of building elements
- BS 8204: Part 1 (1987) to Part 5 (1994) Screeds, bases and insitu floorings
- BS EN28028: 1993 Rubber and/or plastic hose assemblies for airless paint spraying
- CIRIA Paint systems for the protection of construction steelwork (to be published in 1997)

Background

- BS 6100: 1991 Part 1: Section 1.3, Subsection 1.3.7, Glossary of building and civil engineering terms: Finishes (B)

Classification

CAWS Group M, **CEWS** Class V, **CI/SfB** Code (49)u/v

Group D - Building elements and building services
6 - Cleaning of buildings

D6

Read the Introduction (page 9) before using the following guidelines

Scope

- Permanent access equipment.
- Temporary access equipment.
- Roped access.
- Hydraulic platforms (cherry picker).
- Fall/arrest systems (latchways).
- New buildings and existing buildings.
- Ladder access.

Exclusions

- Cleaning of internal spaces, e.g. atria (see D3).

Major Hazards

Refer to the Introduction (page 9) for details of accident types and health risks

Working at height
Dropped objects and substances during cleaning. Falling out of equipment. Falling off edge of building.

Collapse and failure
Provision of safe equipment system for cleaning.

Hazardous materials
Aggressive cleaning materials (use and removal), safe removal of waste process materials.

Weather
Ropes and equipment becoming unstable, tangled or twisted in the wind. Slippery walking surfaces.

Hazardous operations
Repair and maintenance involving cutting, heating gluing or sealing. Unsecured cleaning equipment (e.g. metal bucket).

Access
Safe access and simple operation essential.

GENERAL PLANNING — A

EXCAVATIONS AND FOUNDATIONS — B

PRIMARY STRUCTURE — C

BUILDING ELEMENTS AND BUILDING SERVICES — D 6

CIVIL ENGINEERING — E

A GENERAL PLANNING

B EXCAVATIONS AND FOUNDATIONS

C PRIMARY STRUCTURE

D 6 BUILDING ELEMENTS AND BUILDING SERVICES

E CIVIL ENGINEERING

Specific Hazard Identification

Possible key considerations:

- **Building location**: Are these particular access problems? Do the public have to be protected? Will the site preclude using particular equipment or methods? Is the site exposed?
- **Building form:** How is access to cleaning equipment achieved? Will cleaning operations require oversailing the public or another building? What is the form and geometry of the facade to be cleaned? Are there any overhangs to be cleaned? Is the building of exceptional size?
- **Cleaning strategy:** What, if any, specific cleaning requirements for elements of cladding? What is required frequency of cleaning? Will aggressive/harmful cleaning materials be required?
- **Does replacement and maintenance** of element need to be considered?

Prompts

- Unprotected roof edges
- Trip hazards at roof edges
- Difficult to reach areas
- Special equipment required
- Access to equipment
- Windy site
- Storage of access equipment
- Provision of warning signs

Hazards Consideration in Design

Stage	Considerations and issues	Possible design options to avoid or mitigate hazards identified for cleaning of buildings
Concept Design	• Form of cladding • Cleaning strategy • Cleaning frequency • Materials to be cleaned	• Consider various types of equipment that can reach all surfaces of the building elevation without dangerous manoeuvres (e.g. cradle or cherry pickers). • Avoid the use of materials and finishes that require aggressive cleaning materials. • Entry/exit points for cleaning equipment need to be detailed so that dangerous manoeuvres are avoided (e.g. stepping over the edge of building into cradle). • Consider how cleaning may be eliminated or reduced.
Scheme Design	• Safe working loads • Design life of cladding/finishes • Safe entry/exit • Access to all parts of the facade • Equipment to achieve access require • Review loads from equipment • Power and water supply • Attachment details	• Develop cleaning strategy to provide full and safe coverage of the whole facade using the preferred method (e.g. will the stabilising legs of a cherry picker always be on solid ground?). • Develop strategy for dealing with waste products from cleaning operations.
Detail Design	• Back-up systems • Testing/commission • Service/maintenance	• With the equipment selected for cleaning, ensure that the operatives can attach personal protective equipment to secure points everywhere that cleaning and maintenance is required.

Group D - Building elements and building services
6 - Cleaning of buildings

EXCAVATIONS AND FOUNDATIONS B

BUILDING ELEMENTS AND BUILDING SERVICES D 6

Examples of Risk Mitigation (methods of solution)

ACTION / ISSUE	Falls from building edge when entering cleaning cradle	Collapse of cherry picker
Avoidance Design to avoid identified hazards but beware of introducing others	Use permanently-installed roof-mounted cleaning equipment provided with luffing and slewing jib, so that access to the cradle can occur away from the roof edge.	Provide a flat, solid, clear access round the base of the building as part of the external landscaping design for the building.
Reduction Design to reduce identified hazards but beware of increasing others	Use permanently-installed roof-mounted cleaning equipment with a luffing jib, and provide safe entry points guarded by gates and rails, and with tethering points for the cradle.	Provide designated areas round the base of the building that can be accessed and which are flat, solid and clear. Use permanently-installed roof-mounted cleaning equipment with a
Control Design to provide acceptable safeguards for all remaining identified hazards	luffing jib and provide fall-arrest systems adjacent to cradle access points that can be connected/disconnected when in the cradle.	Specify all-terrain cherry pickers with a known safety record on a variety of surfaces and sub-soil conditions. Provide clear access to the base of the building.

Examples of Risk Mitigation (issues addressed at different stages)

An existing office building in the centre of a major city is to be refurbished and reclad. It has a well-maintained track-mounted trolley supporting a hand- operated cradle to clean two facades and a set of fixed davit arms to support a hand-operated cradle for the other facades. The client would like to refurbish this equipment for future use.

Concept design	Scheme design	Detail design
Manually - operated equipment will be replaced by electrical operation. Review form and geometry of new cladding to establish performance requirements for new equipment.	Ensure safe access routes into the cradle.	Ensure adequate space to allow safe access for maintenance equipment.

An existing shopping centre with a glazed roof over the pedestrian malls has been recently purchased by a new landlord. The roof has been cleaned externally by operators using duck boards and ladders. The new owner wants a new purpose-designed roof access system that will allow the glass to be cleaned without anybody having to stand on the roof.

Concept design	Scheme design	Detail design
Load limitations on the existing glazing framework mean that a travelling gantry supported off the adjacent structure is required.	The travelling gantry is designed to be built adjacent to the mall glazing, and then run on temporary rails on to the permanent rails each side of the mall.	Design gantry so as to provide a safe working area.

Related Issues

References within this document

References	Related issues
A1	Surrounding environment may dictate operation times and frequency of cleaning.
A4	Access to site will dictate how machinery is put up and commissioned.
A4	Access to roof areas will dictate sequencing and protection.
A4,D2	Primary structure will dictate type of fixings, type and span of track, weight of access equipment.
D1-D5	Maintenance, repair and replacement strategy of facade/envelope elements needs to be considered with cleaning.
	External materials will dictate methods and frequency of cleaning.

References for Further Guidance

Primary general references and background information given in Section 4

Primary

- BS 5974: 1990 Code of practice for temporarily installed suspended scaffolds and access equipment
- BS 6037: 1990 Code of practice for permanently installed suspended access equipment
- BS 8213: 1991 Part 1 Code of practice for safety in use and during cleaning of windows and doors
- HSE CIS 5 (revised) Temporarily suspended access cradles and platforms
- HSE CIS 24 Chemical cleaners

Secondary

- BS 2830: 1994 Specification for suspended access equipment
- HSE PM30 Suspended access equipment
- CIRIA Special Publication 71 Graffiti removal and control 1989

Background

- BS 6570: 1986 Code of practice for the selection, care and maintenance of steel wire ropes

Classification

CAWS Group A,   **CEWS** Class A,   **CI/SfB** Code (--)(W2)

Read the Introduction (page 9) before using the following guidelines

GENERAL PLANNING **A**

EXCAVATIONS AND FOUNDATIONS **B**

PRIMARY STRUCTURE **C**

BUILDING ELEMENTS AND BUILDING SERVICES **D 7**

CIVIL ENGINEERING **E**

Scope

- Boiler plant.
- Refrigeration and chiller plant including heat rejection equipment.
- Water treatment plant.
- Air-handling plant.
- Fans and pumps.
- Distribution systems - pipework and ductwork.
- Room units - radiators, fan coils, VAV boxes, etc.
- Gas installations.
- Steam and high temperature hot water installations.
- Smoke ventilation.

Exclusions

- Specialist containment systems - microbiological cabinets, fume cupboards.
- Systems handling hazardous radiological or biological substances.
- Control and control panels (see D8).

Major Hazards

Refer to the Introduction (page 9) for details of accident types and health risks

Falling from heights
Installation, commissioning and maintenance of equipment. Builders work openings

Manual handling
Mechanical equipment is generally large and heavy, or simply bulky.

Hazardous atmospheres/substances
Explosive gas, dusts or vapours, welding fumes, products of combustion, fine fibres, refrigerants, legionella, etc.

Hazardous surfaces
Hot and cold surfaces, projecting parts of equipment (particularly at head and ankle level), sharp edges and ends, tripping and slipping.

Pressurised plant and systems
Refrigeration plant, steam, compressed air systems, medical gases. Decommissioning.

Fixings
Installation and maintenance of equipment fixing vertical, horizontal.

A GENERAL PLANNING

B EXCAVATIONS AND FOUNDATIONS

C PRIMARY STRUCTURE

D 7 BUILDING ELEMENTS AND BUILDING SERVICES

E CIVIL ENGINEERING

Specific Hazard Identification

Possible key considerations:

- **Working height** - How is the installation, commissioning and maintenance of equipment to be carried out?
- **Access for installation, commissioning and maintenance** - What is the frequency at which tasks are carried out (e.g. daily, monthly)?
- **Adequate space** - What are the provisions for mechanical or manual handling of equipment in the plant room and along ingress/egress routes?
- **Hazardous substances** - How will use and storage take place in the installation and operation of mechanical services (e.g. refrigerants ammonia, propane, water treatment chemicals, fine fibres from insulants, microbiological contamination of water services, etc.)?
- **Maintenance** - What are the provisions for the removal and replacement of plant items.
- **Electrical supply to mechanical services**
- **Any others?**

Prompts

- Rooftop locations
- Tripping hazard - low level pipework in plant rooms
- Hot surfaces - boilers and pipework
- Cold surfaces - liquefied gas pipework
- Sharp surfaces - air-handling plant casing, ductwork cladding
- Projecting parts - valve stems and wheels, head level pipes and ducts, etc.
- Pressure systems
- Manual mechanical handling
- Rotating machinery
- Safety valves
- Fixing details
- Welding vs mechanical fixings

Hazards Consideration in Design

Stage	Considerations and issues	Possible design options to avoid or mitigate hazards identified for mechanical services
Concept Design	• Heating/cooling/ventilation strategy • Plant room sizes and locations • Principal distribution routes • Fuel sources and storage • Existing site services	• A building with good thermal characteristics (e.g. external envelope) will often reduce the size and complexity of the mechanical services required. • The handling of large plant items and the amount of space can be reduced by considering modular or decentralised plant. • Location of major plant and main distribution routes for pipes and ducts need careful planning and coordination, particularly riser cores to avoid congestion.
Scheme Design	• Installation strategy • Plant duties and nominal sizes and weights • Pipe and duct distribution • Plant access/egress • Working space for work at all phases • Plant room layouts	• Eliminate or reduce common hazards by thoughtful selection of major plant items - falling from heights (e.g. low level plant), hazardous substances (e.g. non-toxic, non-flammable refrigerants), avoidance of pressurised systems (e.g. low temperature hot water heating systems). • Plan safe handling of plant components along entire access/egress routes. Locate plant rooms to keep these routes as simple as possible, (e.g. heavy and bulky objects at ground level - large boilers, chillers, storage vessels, etc.).

Detail Design	• Handling methods for installation, commissioning and maintenance
	• Temporary access for installation
	• Materials specification
	• Storage of plant and materials
	• Safety interlocks
	• Asbestos
	• Hot working
		• Layout plant rooms with an understanding of the space needed to install, commission and maintain items of plant. Provide ready access to plant items which require regular/frequent maintenance. Provide permanent guarded stairs and catwalks if this is at high level.
		• Consider the manual handling tasks at all phases:
		  - can the task be carried out by one person?
		  - will mechanical handling devices be needed?
		• Layout plantroom to avoid tripping hazards and projecting parts by keeping routes free of pipes and ducts. Plan distribution at high level to reduce low level pipework. Provide step-overs for low level pipes where necessary.

Examples of Risk Mitigation (methods of solution)

ACTION	ISSUE Working at height	Manual handling
Avoidance Design to avoid identified hazards but beware of introducing others	Design to install and maintain from floor level.	Use modular plant which can be easily dismantled.
Reduction Design to reduce identified hazards but beware of increasing others	Key components to be accessed from floor level.	Provide sufficient access and space around the plant.
Control Design to provide acceptable safeguards for all remaining identified hazards	Provide protected catwalks stairs and ladders.	Provide lifting beams for mechanical lifting.

Examples of Risk Mitigation (issues addressed at different stages)

Installation of chiller plant to serve an air conditioned department store with substantial heat gain and long run hours.

Concept design	Scheme design	Detail design
Consider using chillers with air-cooled condensers to avoid contamination of condenser water and handling of water treatment chemicals. Consider using HFC refridgerant to avoid using more toxic or inflammable refrigerant options.	Provide adequate space/access for withdrawal of condenser or evaporator tubes. Access/egress routes to allow the safe handling.	Detail plant room layout to reduce the amount of low-level pipe connecting to the evaporator and condenser. Specify lifting beam above chillers to facilitate removal of heavy plant components. Highlight the risk created by refrigerant leakage.

Distribution pipework and ductwork serving a four pipe fan coil system in a new 10 storey office building.

Concept design	Scheme design	Detail design
Consider access space for installation and maintenance at the cores where several services are located, e.g. ductwork, pipework, electrics, lifts, etc. Segregate service risers to avoid electric shock, fire, explosion hazards.	Co-ordination of horizontal pipework and ductwork in false ceiling voids with structure and other services to provide sufficient space for fixing of brackets for installation and maintenance. Provide clear access to regularly maintained items such as fan coil units, fitters, fire dampers, etc.	Use screwed or flanged connections on pipework to avoid welding. Consider as much prefabrication of pipework and ductwork as possible to reduce the amount work at height.

GENERAL PLANNING — A

EXCAVATIONS AND FOUNDATIONS — B

PRIMARY STRUCTURE — C

BUILDING ELEMENTS AND BUILDING SERVICES — D 7

CIVIL ENGINEERING — E

<table>
<tr><td>**D7**</td><td>**Group D - Building elements and building services**
7 - Mechanical services</td></tr>
</table>

Related Issues

References within this document

References	Related issues
A1	Surrounding environment determine some effects on and from this work.
A4	Access for working at height in an area of existing plant needs clear access and egress routes/systems.
D2	Roofs are often used to house mechanical plant.
D6	Cleaning of buildings will include and/or use mechanical services.
D8	Electrical services almost always interface with mechanical services.
D10	Lifts, escalators and auto walks may also be associated with mechanical services.
E8	Pipes and cables (forming the external infrastructure) will interface with mechanical services.

References for Further Guidance

Primary general references and background information given in Section 4

Primary

- Ministry of Defence, Defence Works Functional Standard, Design and Maintenance Guide 08. Space requirements for plant access, operation and maintenance 1996
- BSRIA Technical Note TN 9/92 - Space and weight allowances for building services plant: Inception stage design 1993
- BSRIA Technical Note TN10/92 - Space allowance for building services: Detail design stage 1992
- BSRIA Application Guide 11/92 - Design for maintainability 1992
- Department of Health NHS Estates, Health Technical Memorandum (HTM) 2023 - Access and accommodation for engineering services 1995
- Department of Health, NHS Estates, Health Technical Memorandum (HTM) 2040 - The control of legionellae in healthcare premises 1993

Secondary

- HSE PM/5 Automatically controlled steam and hot water boilers
- HSE HS(G) 70 Control of legionellosis

Background

- BS 8313: 1989 Code of practice for accommodation of building services in ducts

Classification

CAWS Group S&T, **CEWS** Class Z, **CI/SfB** Code (54)/(59)

A GENERAL PLANNING

B EXCAVATIONS AND FOUNDATIONS

C PRIMARY STRUCTURE

D 7 BUILDING ELEMENTS AND BUILDING SERVICES

E CIVIL ENGINEERING

Read the Introduction (page 9) before using the following guidelines

Scope

- HV equipment and transformers.
- LV switchgear and components.
- Uninterruptible power supplies (UPS).
- Generators.
- Lightning protection.
- Fire and security alarm systems.
- Lighting and power cabling.
- Emergency lighting.
- Mechanical plant supplies.

Exclusions

- Large-scale power generation plant and distribution systems.
- Areas designated as having potentially explosive atmospheres - "hazardous areas".
- Temporary services during construction.

Major Hazards

Refer to the Introduction (page 9) for details of accident types and health risks

Confined working spaces
Installation, maintenance, commissioning.

Falling from heights
Installation and maintenance of equipment, falling into pits (e.g. switchrooms). Builders work openings.

Manual handling of plant
Large and heavy switchgear components, transformers, generators, etc.

Hazardous surfaces
Hot surfaces, projecting parts of equipment (particularly at head and ankle level), sharp edges and ends, tripping and slipping.

Hazardous atmospheres/ substances
Insulating oils from transformers or HV switchgear, acids from batteries, hydrogen from charging batteries, etc.

Fixings
Installation and maintenance of fixings for equipment, on walls or in floor/ceiling zones.

GENERAL PLANNING — A

EXCAVATIONS AND FOUNDATIONS — B

PRIMARY STRUCTURE — C

BUILDING ELEMENTS AND BUILDING SERVICES — D8

CIVIL ENGINEERING — E

A — GENERAL PLANNING

B — EXCAVATIONS AND FOUNDATIONS

C — PRIMARY STRUCTURE

D8 — BUILDING ELEMENTS AND BUILDING SERVICES

E — CIVIL ENGINEERING

Specific Hazard Identification

Possible key considerations:

- **New build or refurbishment** - identify if the power supply to the building will be "live" during any electrical works?
- **Working height** - how is the installation and maintenance of equipment to be carried out, (e.g. replacement of lamps)?
- **Access for installation and maintenance** - What is the frequency needed for access to equipment (daily, monthly, etc.)?
- **Adequate space** - what are the provisions for mechanical/ manual handling of equipment in equipment rooms and along access/egress routes through the building?
- **Maintenance** - what are the provisions for removal and replacement of equipment.
- **Any others ?**

Prompts

- Equipment located at high level or in false ceiling voids
- Sharp surfaces - electrical tray work and conduits.
- Manual handling (e.g. removal of switchgear truck)
- Hazardous substances (e.g transformer oil)
- Hot surfaces - generator engines and flues
- Fixing details

Hazards Consideration in Design

Stage	Considerations and issues	Possible design options to avoid or mitigate hazards identified for electrical services
Concept Design	• Electrical supply strategy • Equipment room sizes and locations • Construction requirements - small plant, lighting and plant, UPS • Principal distribution routes • Existing site services • Installation strategy • Equipment and switchgear capacity, nominal sizes and weights	• Maximum size of low-voltage supply may be determined by electricity company. Maintenance of high voltage systems require specially-certificated personnel. • Locate main equipment rooms at outer walls of buildings, where possible, to allow heavy equipment to be placed in one lift from lorry to final position. • Locate principal distribution routes away from plant rooms used by other services (if possible). • Route external cable trenches away from existing routes to avoid coincident excavations. • Avoid whenever possible carrying out electrical work on "live" services.
Scheme Design	• Main risers and sub-circuit routes • Plant access/egress routes • Switchgear and equipment room layouts	• Ensure sufficient space to install largest item of plant safely. • Use dedicated risers and routes for electrical services wherever possible so the electrical installers are not put in danger from other (unfamiliar) services.
Detail Design	• Handling methods for installation and maintenance • Temporary access for installation • Materials specification • Separation of services • Earthing and bonding	• Locate equipment with sufficient working space so emergency egress is not obstructed. • Provide lifting beams where heavy parts need to be lifted for maintenance. • Ensure any temporary access for installation does not require electrical contractor to dismantle pipes or rebuild a wall. • Wherever possible, avoid materials that may require special handling or protection during disposal.

Examples of Risk Mitigation (methods of solution)

ACTION \ ISSUE	Hazardous substances	Manual handling during installation
Avoidance Design to avoid identified hazards but beware of introducing others	Consider use of non combustible materials for all electrical equipment to guard against electrical/construction fires.	Design modular switchboards with smaller components.
Reduction Design to reduce identified hazards but beware of increasing others	Specify fire retardant/low smoke insulants on cables instead of PVC.	Design access routes with sufficient space for mechanical handling devices.
Control Design to provide acceptable safeguards for all remaining identified hazards	Co-ordinate with other designers to incorporate smoke vents/ventilation in areas where work will take place.	Incorporate lifting beams for electrical gear into primary structure.

Examples of Risk Mitigation (issues addressed at different stages)

In designing the mains supply to an urban office building it becomes apparent that building loading requires a new HV supply. The only space available for transformer is in the basement adjacent to the car park area.

Concept design	Scheme design	Detail design
Location presents considerable fire risk so use a dry transformer with SF6 or vacuum switchgear. Put all cabling at high level. Access to the new switchroom will be via the car park - incorporate security measures to prevent unauthorised access.	Design to allow HV switchgear and transformer to be installed together in one room. Allow space for removal of HV switchgear and rear access to LV switchgear.	Specify sealed batteries for HV backup to avoid hazard of explosive gasses from charging unsealed batteries.

Large incoming supply arrangement with multiple transformers and both high voltage and low voltage switchgear.

Concept design	Scheme design	Detail design
Consider installing transformers in separate vaults to allow safe working on one while others are still energised. Provide separate rooms for LV and HV switchgear.	Design system with comprehensive electrical interlocking and earthing facilities to ensure no parts can become live unexpectedly. Ensure the interlocks prevent the possibility of earthing live sections or "backfeeding" through the transformers.	Ensure specification of all switchgear includes security provisions, e.g. padlocks.

GENERAL PLANNING — A

EXCAVATIONS AND FOUNDATIONS — B

PRIMARY STRUCTURE — C

BUILDING ELEMENTS AND BUILDING SERVICES — D8

CIVIL ENGINEERING — E

A GENERAL PLANNING

B EXCAVATIONS AND FOUNDATIONS

C PRIMARY STRUCTURE

D 8 BUILDING ELEMENTS AND BUILDING SERVICES

E CIVIL ENGINEERING

Related Issues

References within this document

References	Related issues
A4	Access is a crucial issue for installing or maintaining electrical services.
D7	Mechanical services will (almost) always require electrical services.
D10	Lifts and escalators will be electrically driven.
E8	Pipes and cables from external infrastructure will interface with electrical services.

References for Further Guidance

Primary general references and background information given in Section 4

Primary

- Ministry of Defence, Defence Works Functional Standard, Design and Maintenance Guide 08. Space requirements for plant access, operation and maintenance 1996
- BSRIA Technical Note TN 9/92 - Space and weight allowances for building services plant: Inception stage design 1993
- BSRIA Technical Note TN10/92 - Space allowance for building services: Detail design stage 1992
- BSRIA Application Guide 11/92 - Design for maintainability 1992
- Department of Health NHS Estates, Health Technical Memorandum (HTM) 2023 - Access and accommodation for engineering services 1995
- Department of Health, NHS Estates, Health Technical Memorandum (HTM) 2040 - The control of legionellae in healthcare premises 1993

Secondary

- HSE HS(R)25 Memorandum of guidance on the Electricity at Work Regulations
- BS 8313: 1989 Code of practice for accommodation of building services in ducts

Background

- BS 7671: 1992 Requirements for Electrical Installations

Classification

CAWS Group V,   **CEWS** Class Z,   **CI/SfB** Code (6-)

Read the Introduction (page 9) before using the following guidelines

Scope

- Cold water supply.
- Hot water supply.
- Water treatment plant.
- Surface water and foul drainage.
- Waste and refuse disposal systems.
- Above - ground sanitary systems, soil waste and vents.
- Water and gas fire extinguishing systems.

Exclusions

- Commercial incinerator plant.
- Chemical waste and drainage systems.
- Sewage treatment plants.

Major Hazards

Refer to the Introduction (page 9) for details of accident types and health risks

Falls from heights
During installation, commissioning and maintenance of equipment. Falling into excavations.

Deep excavations
Collapse of excavation, working in confined spaces, hazardous gases.

Access
Routes to equipmnt.
High level equipment.
Equipment in holes or tunnels.

Manual handling
Tanks and other public health plant are generally large and heavy or bulky.

Hazardous atmospheres/substances
Explosive atmospheres (e.g methane), gas, legionella.
Suffocating atmospheres (e.g. carbon dioxide).
Poisonous atmospheres (e.g. hydrogen sulphide).

Hazardous surfaces
Projecting parts of equipment (particularly at head and ankle level), sharp edges and ends, tripping and slipping.

Right margin tabs:
GENERAL PLANNING — A
EXCAVATIONS AND FOUNDATIONS — B
PRIMARY STRUCTURE — C
BUILDING ELEMENTS AND BUILDING SERVICES — D 9
CIVIL ENGINEERING — E

Specific Hazard Identification

Possible key considerations:

- **Working height** - How is the installation and maintenance of equipment to be carried out?

- **Access for installation and maintenance** - What is the frequency at which tasks are carried out, (e.g. daily, monthly, etc.)?

- **Adequate space** - What are the provisions for mechanical or manual handling of equipment in the plant room and along access/egress routes through the building?

- **Hazardous substances** - How will the use and storage take place in the installation and operation of mechanical services (e.g. water treatment chemicals, fine fibres from insulants, etc.)? Is there risk of microbiological contamination of water services?

- **Maintenance** - What are the provisions for the removal and replacement of items of plant?

- **Any others?**

Prompts

- Roof top locations
- Tripping hazard - low - level pipework in plant rooms
- Hot surfaces - calorifiers and pipework
- Sharp surfaces - cladding
- Projecting parts - valve stems and wheels, head level pipes and ducts, etc.
- Pressure systems
- Manual handling.
- Fixing details
- Purge existing systems

Hazards Consideration in Design

Stage	Considerations and issues	Possible design options to avoid or mitigate hazards identified for public health services
Concept Design		• Locate bulk water storage tanks in plant rooms with minimum heat gain. Establish principal distribution routes which allow safe manoeuvring of large diameter heavy pipework, during installation and renewal. • Allow access around proposed plant when assessing plant room sizes. These can be refined later. • Establish preliminary information on existing site services.
Scheme Design	• Water supply/waste/fire extinguishing - systems strategies • Plant room sizes and locations • Principal distribution routes of all services • Water sources and storage • Existing site services • Installation strategy • Plant weights • Plant access/egress routes • Working space for installation • Handling methods for installation and maintenance • Materials specification	• Specify sectional tanks for bulk water storage, for ease of handling. • Allow working space around plant and tanks for installation and maintenance. • Provide working platforms in risers where floor slab is not continued through. • Locate all existing site services before laying out external mains and drainage. Keep excavations clear of existing structures and services. • Minimise depth of excavations
Detail Design		• Consider access for lifting equipment which may be required for heavy high level services. • Specify drainage sump pumps which can be maintained at floor level. • Consider (lightweight) plastic materials for larger diameter high-level pipework. • Locate drainage access points where they can be easily and safely maintained. • Locate valves on pipelines at points of safe permanent access. • Ensure safe routes available for replacement of plant. • Holes in GRP tanks to be formed at works to avoid drilling on site.

Examples of Risk Mitigation (methods of solution)

ACTION \ ISSUE	Installing plant at high level	Manual handling during dismantling
Avoidance Design to avoid identified hazards but beware of introducing others	Design to install and maintain plant at floor level.	Use modular plant which can be dismantled into manageable sections.
Reduction Design to reduce identified hazards but beware of increasing others	Key components to be accessed from floor level.	Provide sufficient access and space around the plant to allow mechanical handling devices to be used.
Control Design to provide acceptable safeguards for all remaining identified hazards	Provide protected catwalks stairs and ladders to high level plant.	Provide lifting eyes and/or runways for lifting plant with manual assistance.

Examples of Risk Mitigation (issues addressed at different stages)

Large diameter drainage run is to be routed through 5m high plantroom at high level.

Concept design	Scheme design	Detail design
Plan route which will have access from below for lifting equipment. This could involve mechanical lifting devices. Avoid routes over arears where future plant might be installed to aid replacement	Consider plastic pipes rather than cast iron, to ease manual handling. For cast iron pipes, specify mechanical joints.	Locate cleaning access doors where they can be accessed from a gantry or permanent catwalk. Where possible, avoid high level cleaning access points by extending access through the floor slab and carry out maintenance from the floor above.

Drainage outfall from a building is along a main traffic route from office car park.

Concept design	Scheme design	Detail design
Route drainage (where possible) below pavement or landscaping. Avoid deep excavation adjacent to existing structures.	Locate manholes away from site roads. Where manholes cannot be avoided in roadway, locate them to one side. If sufficient depth is available, use "side entry" manhole with access shaft in pavement.	In deep manholes use ladders rather than step irons for safer access. Where large heavy duty covers are required, consider multiple covers to reduce manual handling load. Where outfall pipe from manhole is 600mm diameter or greater, fit safety chain across outlet.

GENERAL PLANNING — A

EXCAVATIONS AND FOUNDATIONS — B

PRIMARY STRUCTURE — C

BUILDING ELEMENTS AND BUILDING SERVICES — D 9

CIVIL ENGINEERING — E

Related Issues

References within this document

References	Related issues
A4	Access for maintenance and commissioning.
B2	Deep basements and shafts.
B3	Trenches for services.
D2	Roofs - rainwater drainage.
D8	Electrical services connect to equipment and plant.
E8	Pipes and cables.

References for Further Guidance

Primary general references and background information given in Section 4

Primary

- Ministry of Defence, Defence Works Functional Standard, Design and Maintenance Guide 08. Space requirements for plant access, operation and maintenance 1996
- BSRIA Technical Note TN 9/92 - Space and weight allowances for building services plant: Inception stage design 1993
- BSRIA Technical Note TN10/92 - Space allowance for building services: Detail design stage 1992
- BSRIA Application Guide 11/92 - Design for maintainability 1992
- Department of Health NHS Estates, Health Technical Memorandum (HTM) 2023 - Access and accommodation for engineering services 1995
- Department of Health, NHS Estates, Health Technical Memorandum (HTM) 2040 - The control of legionellae in healthcare premises 1993
- HSE HS(G) 70 Control of legionellosis.

Secondary

- BS 8313: 1989 Code of practice for accommodation of building services in ducts
- BS 5572: 1994 Code of practice for sanitation pipework
- BS 6367: 1983 Code of practice for drainage of roofs and paved areas

Background

- BS 8005: 1987 Sewerage Part 1 Guide to new sewerage construction
- BS 8301: 1985 Code of practice for building drainage
- Building Regulations 1991. Approved document G - Sanitary conveniences and washing facilities, bathrooms and HWS storage 1992
- BS 6700: 1987 Services supplying water for domestic use within buildings
- Institute of Plumbing - Plumbing engineering services design guide
- Water Research Centre Sewers for adoption 1995

Classification

CAWS Group R&S, **CEWS** Class Z, **CI/SfB** Codes (52)/(53)

Read the Introduction (page 9) before using the following guidelines

Scope

- Traction lifts.
- Hydraulic lifts.
- Escalators.
- Autowalks.

Exclusions

- Temporary mobile platforms, scissor lifts.
- General mechanical handling equipment, e.g. document handling, baggage handling.

Major Hazards

Refer to the Introduction (page 9) for details of accident types and health risks

Collapse
Heavy equipment on un-propped floors.

Falling from heights
Falling into pits and shafts. Access to lift motor room.
Installation, commissioning and maintenance of equipment.

Manual handling
Large and heavy items of equipment. Space for installation, commissioning and maintenance.

Hazardous surfaces
Projecting parts of equipment (particularly at head and ankle level), sharp edges and ends, tripping and slipping.

Hazardous substances
Dusts and vapours, bottled gases, fibrous dust, asbestos, hydraulic oils, etc.
Working in confined spaces.

Installation
Noise and vibration, entanglement, trapping, crushing, cutting by moving parts.

Specific Hazard Identification

Possible key considerations:

- **Insulation, isolation, overload protection and earthing of equipment** - What provisions have been made?
- **Working height** - How is the installation and maintenance of equipment to be carried out?
- **Access for installation, commissioning and maintenance** - What is the frequency at which access will be required to equipment (daily, monthly)?
- **Adequate space** - What are provisions for mechanical or manual handling of equipment in equipment rooms and along ingress/egress routes through the building?
- **Maintenance** - What are the provisions for the removal and replacement of items of equipment?
- **Hazardous substances** - What provision has been made for the use, movement and storage of hazardous substances?
- **Any others?**

Prompts

- Working at high level
- Working in lift shafts
- Sharp surfaces - equipment casing, cladding, etc.
- Manual handling
- Hazardous substances e.g. hydraulic oil
- Projecting parts - valves, wheels, pipes and ducts
- Fire risks - shafts and machine rooms
- Hot surfaces - motors and hydraulic tanks

Hazards Consideration in Design

Stage	Considerations and issues	Possible design options to avoid or mitigate hazards identified for lifts, escalators, etc.
Concept Design		• Consider the time-scale of operation and delivery of plant, avoid duplication of tasks such as striking and re-erection of scaffolding in lift wells. • Consider alternative routes for access. Provide sufficient working space for installation, commissioning and maintenance.
Scheme Design	• Location of lifts and motor rooms • Scope of works • Familiar work • Access • Installation sequences • Lift equipment types • Handling of equipment components • Protection • Installation, commissioning and maintenance procedures • Space for services • Handling of equipment • Finishes • Positioning • Temporary supports	• Specify equipment that is compact in design to allow for easy handling and placing in position. • Allow for suitable permanent/temporary lifting facilities (marked with SWL) for final positioning of plant. • Consider components which are pre-fabricated and delivered to site as packaged units. • Include provision for delivery and handling of components on congested sites.
Detail Design		• Allow for future repair or renewal of equipment, by providing suitable lifting access/egress routes for plant and personnel. • Allow for adequate safety harness attachments for personnel working at heights within the lift well. • If mechanical handling is necessary, incorporate into the design provision for mechanical lifting and handling.

Examples of Risk Mitigation (methods of solution)

ACTION	ISSUE **Maintenance in confined spaces**
Avoidance Design to avoid identified hazards but beware of introducing others	Specify long life, sealed components: These to be replaced rather than maintained.
Reduction Design to reduce identified hazards but beware of increasing others	Specify minimal maintenance components.
Control Design to provide acceptable safeguards for all remaining identified hazards	Provide sufficient space for maintenance tasks.

Examples of Risk Mitigation (issues addressed at different stages)

The installation of an escalator into a building. A compact escalator system is proposed which can be delivered in one piece to reduce programme requirements.

Concept design	Scheme design	Detail design
The overall concept for the method of installation should be planned.	Ensure adequate space allowed for installation.	Further consideration of the sequence of installation. Identify specific hazards due to the building structure.

Panoramic lift installation to serve a department store

Concept design	Scheme design	Detail design
The lift should be designed so that it can be installed in a completed form, or consideration to be given to access/egress routes to allow safe handling of components.	Panoramic lifts use laminated glass, for walls, ceilings and doors. Provision should be made for the safe handling of this material and future cleaning requirements.	The design should allow for safe cleaning of the glass. Allocate one floor, (e.g. ground level), where all-round access can be arranged. Ensure adequate depth of well to allow safe maintenance.

GENERAL PLANNING — A

EXCAVATIONS AND FOUNDATIONS — B

PRIMARY STRUCTURE — C

BUILDING ELEMENTS AND BUILDING SERVICES — D 10

CIVIL ENGINEERING — E

A GENERAL PLANNING

B EXCAVATIONS AND FOUNDATIONS

C PRIMARY STRUCTURE

D 10 BUILDING ELEMENTS AND BUILDING SERVICES

E CIVIL ENGINEERING

Related Issues

References within this document

References	Related issues
D3	Roofs may house lift motor rooms.
D7	Mechanical services interact closely with the installation and maintenance of vertical transportation components.
D8	Electrical services need to be considered for the installation and maintenance of lifts and escalators, also emergency lighting.
D9	Public health services - often impinge on the installation and maintenance of lifts and escalators.
	Fire engineering needs to be considered for fire-fighting lifts.

References for Further Guidance

Primary general references and background information given in Section 4

Primary

- BS EN 115: 1995 Safety rules for the construction and installation of escalators and passenger conveyors
- National Association of Lift Manufacturers. Principles of planning and programming a lift installation 1994
- National Association of Lift Manufacturers/CIBSE - Guidance on the management and maintenance of lifts and escalators.

Secondary

- CIBSE Guide D Transportation in buildings 1993.

Background

- BS 5655 Lifts and service lifts: Parts 3 to 12 (1989)
- BS 7255: 1989 Code of practice for the safe working on lifts
- BS 5588: Part 5: 1991 Code of practice for fire fighting stairs and lifts.

Classification

CAWS Group X, **CI//SfB** Code (66)

Read the Introduction (page 9) before using the following guidelines

Scope

- Civil engineering construction sites.
- More detail on selected civil engineering operations is given in work sectors E2 to E8 as well as work sectors in groups B and C.

Exclusions

NONE

Major Hazards

Refer to the Introduction (page 9) for details of accident types and health risks

Buried/crushed/trapped
Collapsed excavation of service trench/foundation.
Backfilling in confined space.
Falsework/formwork collapse.

Falls
Awkward access/egress.
Inadequate working space.
Unstable platforms.

Health hazards
Chemicals.
Asbestos.
Gases.
Water-borne diseases and contamination.
Contaminated ground.
Manual handling.

Machinery and transport
Site traffic and plant.
Public highway traffic adjacent to site.
Unloading materials and equipment.

Services
Power cables (underground and overhead).
Fuel and gas pipelines. Sewers.
High pressure mains water.

Ground movement
Landslips, flooding.
Subsidence.
Fractured services.

Side tabs:
- A — GENERAL PLANNING
- B — EXCAVATIONS AND FOUNDATIONS
- C — PRIMARY STRUCTURE
- D — BUILDING ELEMENTS AND BUILDING SERVICES
- E 1 — CIVIL ENGINEERING

A GENERAL PLANNING

B EXCAVATIONS AND FOUNDATIONS

C PRIMARY STRUCTURE

D BUILDING ELEMENTS AND BUILDING SERVICES

E 1 CIVIL ENGINEERING

Specific Hazard Identification

Possible key considerations:

- **Site survey** - What is the history of site? Is there contamination from previous use?
- **Ground survey** - What significant foundation problems will be encountered?
- **Working room** - What is the most appropriate plant?
- **Flooding** - What is the likelihood of a flood occurring?
- **Services** - Where are they? What measures to divert or protect?
- **Any others?**

Prompts

- Previous site use
- Waste disposal
- Access/egress
- Adjacent property
- Adjacent operations
- Construction planning
- Noise/vibration/dust.
- On-site storag
- Confined spaces/ventilation

Hazards Consideration in Design

Stage	Considerations and issues	Possible design options to avoid or mitigate hazards identified for general civil engineering
Concept Design	• Why this site? • Site history • Affected local buildings • Depth of foundations • Location of services • Access routes	• Review the practicalities of other layouts or routes with fewer/less serious hazards. • Choose a massing arrangement of structures which will allow wide battered excavations. • Design to consider effect on local environment (e.g. access/egress, noise and vibration, lighting), not just the convenience and value of the project. • Assess the possible benefits from further site investigation or specialist surveys. • Avoid disturbance of existing services.
Scheme Design	• Ground conditions • Topography • Drainage/hydrology • Working space • Plant/machinery • Excavation support • Spoil/contamination • Drainage	• Consider drainage measures to improve the stability of excavations. • Ensure that construction methods are practical in relation to the working space available.
Detail Design	• Advance works • Protection of public • Maintenance • Cleaning	• Design to minimise excavation depths. • Consider appropriate methods for groundwater control. • Consider an enabling works contract to protect or divert services. • Include "systems" for future safe working procedures for maintenance, cleaning and possibly demolition phases.

Group E - Civil engineering
1 - General civil engineering - including small works

Examples of Risk Mitigation (methods of solution)

ACTION \ ISSUE	Major services crossing the site	Rights of way
Avoidance Design to avoid identified hazards but beware of introducing others	Plan the location of major buildings/structures to avoid the route of major services.	Avoid established right of way.
Reduction Design to reduce identified hazards but beware of increasing others	Protect or divert services.	Redirect highways and footpaths temporarily.
Control Design to provide acceptable safeguards for all remaining identified hazards	Specify suitable identification of services.	On site measures will be managed by Principal Contractor.

Examples of Risk Mitigation (issues addressed at different stages)

A small group of residential dwellings is to be constructed on the site of a disused small sewage works, adjacent to a river. Proposals are required to deal with the residual site contaminants.

Concept design	Scheme design	Detail design
Complete site inspection to identify contamination in relation to new dwellings. Identify history and construction records of site. Locate services.	Confirm extent of contamination and ground water details by site investigation. Consider methods to contain/remove contaminants. Identify ground dewatering methods, excavation, drainage requirements, etc.	Develop details for foundations and drainage which minimise ground disturbance.

A flood alleviation scheme requires surface water storage capacity under a residential street.

Concept design	Scheme design	Detail design
Find the optimum balance between cross-sectional area and length of sewer to allow construction access while retaining pedestrian access to the houses.	Determine the position in the road which minimises the disruption and interfaces with existing services.	Locate penstock taps and main chamber access covers in a traffic island or wide pavement for safer access during maintenance.

GENERAL PLANNING **A**

EXCAVATIONS AND FOUNDATIONS **B**

PRIMARY STRUCTURE **C**

BUILDING ELEMENTS AND BUILDING SERVICES **D**

CIVIL ENGINEERING **E 1**

Related Issues

References within this document

References	Related issues
A1,A2	Local environment protection is required from the hazards associated with any construction or demolition work.
A3	Ground investigations should be related to the project to be constructed.
A4	Access/egress routes may affect the site and hence the construction materials to be used and the frequency of deliveries.
A5	Site layout will be determined by the project to be constructed on the site available and plant to be used. If site restricted, hazards of construction could be accentuated.
C1-C4	Concrete construction
C5,C6	Structural Steelwork construction
E2,E3	Railways/roads/water, adjacent construction work should include safe distances and suitable protection for persons on site.

References for Further Guidance

Primary general references and background information given in Section 4

Primary

- CIRIA Special Publication 57 Handling of materials on site 1988
- CIRIA Report 97 Trenching practice 1992
- HSE HS(G) 47 Avoiding danger from underground services
- HSE GS6 Avoidance of danger from overhead electric lines
- HSE HS(G) 66 Protection of workers and the general public during the development of contaminated land
- HSE CIS 36 Silica

Secondary

- HSE GS5 Entry into confined spaces
- HSE GS29 Parts 1 to 4 Health and safety in demolition work
- HSE GS28 Parts 1 to 4 Safe erection of structures
- CIRIA Report 130 Methane: its occurrence and hazards in construction 1993
- CIRIA Report 113 Control of groundwater for temporary works 1988

Background

- BS 6031: 1981 Code of Practice for Earthworks
- BS 8002 : 1994 Earth Retaining Structures
- Tomlinson, Foundation design and construction 1995

Classification

CEWS Classes A-Z, **CI/SfB** Code (--)1

Read the Introduction (page 9) before using the following guidelines

Scope

- Existing roads - motorways, dual carriageways, all-purpose roads in rural, urban and city centre locations.
- New road construction, including motorway widening.

Exclusions

- Roads in tunnels.
- Roads on viaducts.
- Temporary roads.

Major Hazards

Refer to the Introduction (page 9) for details of accident types and health risks

Traffic
Working adjacent to live traffic. Traffic management in temporary conditions. Intrusion of runaway vehicles.

Falls
Equipment dropped from overhead structure/top of retaining wall.
Falls into route of traffic.

Plant and machinery
Collisions between construction plant, highway traffic and pedestrians.
Crossing and slewing over the highway.

Services
Excavation of pipes, drains and cables.
Collision with overhead cables.

Buried/crushed/trapped
Collapse of excavation for drainage or services.
Landslip triggered by excavation near toe of batter/surcharge.

Health hazards
Damaged hearing.
Vibration white finger.
Inhalation of dust and solvents.
Contaminated land.

GENERAL PLANNING   **A**

EXCAVATIONS AND FOUNDATIONS   **B**

PRIMARY STRUCTURE   **C**

BUILDING ELEMENTS AND BUILDING SERVICES   **D**

CIVIL ENGINEERING   **E2**

A GENERAL PLANNING

B EXCAVATIONS AND FOUNDATIONS

C PRIMARY STRUCTURE

D BUILDING ELEMENTS AND BUILDING SERVICES

E 2 CIVIL ENGINEERING

Specific Hazard Identification

Possible key considerations:

- **Site survey** - What site contamination is present?
- **Ground investigation** - What water table and slope stability problems exist?
- **Access** - How is safe access and egress provided?
- **Working room** - How can sufficient space for safety zones and plant/equipment be allocated?
- **Traffic management** - How can the design assist traffic and pedestrian management?
- **General public** - What site security arrangements are required?
- **Services - Location?** What measures are needed to protect?
- **Any others?**

Prompts

- Access Routes
- Traffic diversions
- Lane closures/signage
- Deliveries/waste disposal
- Utilities/services
- Weather
- Road/street lighting
- Protect pedestrians

Hazards Consideration in Design

Stage	Considerations and issues	Possible design options to avoid or mitigate hazards identified for working adjacent to and maintaining roads
Concept Design	• Site history • Urban/rural location • Access routes • Services • Hydrology	• Consider whether further soil testing/investigation will enable a better prediction of temporary slope stability. • Consider location of major overhead or underground services with respect to expected working methods. • The route location and type of road should be considered in relation to safe access and delivery of materials to the site.
Scheme Design	• Lane rental • Ground conditions • Road geometry • Drainage • Plant and machinery • Working space • Sequencing • Advance works • Traffic management • Interaction with existing traffic • Pavement • Earthworks • Noise • Maintenance	• For easier access and movement of machinery, consider advance drainage works, watercourse diversions, etc. • Check that the chosen temporary diversion of traffic causes the least trouble elsewhere. • Design to facilitate staged construction, so that traffic is not diverted elsewhere.
Detail Design		• Avoid the (temporary) diversion of services in advance of works commencing. • Traffic management measures, temporary signage and lighting to be incorporated into partially complete works. • Design to reduce frequency of maintenance, particularly for the more heavily trafficked routes. • Programme the contract periods to avoid seasonal peak traffic flows.

Examples of Risk Mitigation (methods of solution)

ACTION / ISSUE	Working adjacent to high speed traffic	Land slide/ embankment slip
Avoidance Design to avoid identified hazards but beware of introducing others	Divert all traffic or close one carriageway.	Minimum or zero excavation required by using piled foundations and setting the structure at a higher level.
Reduction Design to reduce identified hazards but beware of increasing others	Divert Heavy Goods Vehicles (HGV) only. Add a lane closure to create a buffer zone.	Grade the embankment or cutting to a shallower angle before excavation for other works.
Control Design to provide acceptable safeguards for all remaining identified hazards	Specify concrete barriers.	Stabilise the slope by contingency methods (such as soil nailing) and drainage, as required in response to movement monitoring.

Examples of Risk Mitigation (issues addressed at different stages)

A stretch of uneven road surface requires emergency repair.

Concept design	Scheme design	Detail design
The exposure of workers was assessed for both temporary repair and complete carriageway reconstruction. Possible road closure periods identified.	Investigations organised ahead of repairs to reduce the possibility of extra unforeseen works. Roadwork contracts on neighbouring routes were accelerated or delayed to minimise overall disruption.	Materials were chosen which could be laid in narrow strips to give maximum flexibility of construction planning.

A single carriageway is to be converted to a two-lane dual carriageway.

Concept design	Scheme design	Detail design
Consider new routes on separate land, parallel land take or confining work to existing corridor.	Route details to consider safe access points for plant and operatives.	New road lighting designed to reduce the need for temporary lighting during construction.

GENERAL PLANNING — A

EXCAVATIONS AND FOUNDATIONS — B

PRIMARY STRUCTURE — C

BUILDING ELEMENTS AND BUILDING SERVICES — D

CIVIL ENGINEERING — E2

Related Issues

References within this document

References	Related issues
A1	Local environment should be protected from the hazards associated with roadworks.
A3	Ground investigations should include testing for toxic materials, soil density and gases, as well as stability and groundwater details.
A4	Access/egress routes at the site should be kept clean, clear and suitable for emergency services.
A5	Site layout should be suitable for the working space available and plant anticipated to be used on the site.
C1-C4	Concrete materials brought to site in bulk for batching will require designated storage and batching areas.
C5,C6	Special Access routes for large prefabricated elements need to be planned.
E1	General civil engineering often involves working adjacent to roads
E4,E5	Bridge construction and maintenance
E6,E7	Working near water introduces the hazards of drowning and flooding.
E8	Pipes and cables are most often installed adjacent to roads.

References for Further Guidance

Primary general references and background information given in Section 4

Primary

- Department of Transport (DoT)/Federation of Civil Engineering Contractors (FCEC), Planning for safety: guidance notes for the health and safety of workers at in-service motorway roadworks sites.
- DoT/CSS Notes for Guidance on Safety at Roadworks 1994
- HSE CIS 36 - Silica

Secondary

- DoT Safety at Streetworks and Roadworks: A Code of Practice, 1993
- CIRIA Report 113 Control of a groundwater for temporary works 1988

Background

- DoT Chapter 8 Traffic Signs Manual

Classification

CEWS Class R,   **CI/SfB** Code (--)12

Read the Introduction (page 9) before using the following guidelines

Scope

- Working adjacent to, and over operational railways.
- Maintenance work on operational railways.

Note: Extensive and strict procedures apply when working in connection with operational railways to ensure safety of the workers and general public. The clear definition of the work area with respect to the line is of paramount importance. This will be determined by the respective operator (e.g. Railtrack, London Underground Ltd, Docklands Light Railway, etc.)

Exclusions

- Railways in tunnels.
- Maintenance depots.
- Specialist trackwork and electrification work.
- Private railways.

Major Hazards

Refer to the Introduction (page 9) for details of accident types and health risks

Struck by moving trains
Organisation of personnel and material handling not in accordance with established safety procedures.

Lifting failures
Electrocution (overhead or third rail). Damage to signals, signal controls and communications.

Ground instability
Rock falls into cuttings. Embankment slips.

Trains collide with plant
Encroachment into permanent way envelope by plant/machinery. Dropped equipment/components.

Falls, trips and slips
Bridge maintenance. Uneven surfaces. Steep cuttings and embankments. Access to services.

Health hazards
Noise and vibration. Contaminated land. Asbestos, oils.

A GENERAL PLANNING

B EXCAVATIONS AND FOUNDATIONS

C PRIMARY STRUCTURE

D BUILDING ELEMENTS AND BUILDING SERVICES

E 3 CIVIL ENGINEERING

Specific Hazard Identification

Possible key considerations:

- **Electricity** - How are lines electrified (overhead and electric, 3rd or 4th Rail)?
- **Working Space** - What size of plant is to be used? Is there sufficient space?
- **Site survey/Records** - Where are cable, signals cabinets, other railway furniture located?
- **Track geometry** - How will this affect work methods?
- **Train movement** - What train movements have to be maintained?
- **Track possessions** - Will possessions be necessary or possible?
- **Track operator** - What are the requirements of the operator?
- **Operations/windows** Track possession or full closure?
- **Any others?**

Prompts

- Track working rules and procedures
- Codes of practice
- Contamination
- Protection of public
- Noise/vibration
- Weather/temperature
- Material storage
- Emergency procedures
- Access
- General public

Hazards Consideration in Design

Stage	Considerations and issues	Possible design options to avoid or mitigate hazards identified for working adjacent to, and working on railways
Concept Design	• Historical records • Site access restrictions • Underground and overground services • Maintenance • Location	• Consider design options in which the proximity of the railway has least effect. • The type and frequency of rail traffic may prohibit or restrict certain methods of construction. • Design for minimum track possessions or consider full closure with train diversions. • Check whether the safety of rail passengers will be impaired in anyway. Ensure separation of public and construction work.
Scheme Design	• Working space • Ground conditions • Drainage • Night working • Access • Working at stations • Safe refuge areas • Disposal of waste • Cable protection	• Examine the possibility of modification to cuttings and embankments to improve working space or storage areas. • Consider night working and removal of power supply to overhead lines or electrified rails. • Determine the activities which require track possession and for how long. • Provide access to control boxes etc. other than along the track. • Allow for frequent areas of safety alongside the track.
Detail Design	• Track possessions • Delivery of materials • General Public • Other transport systems	• Consider the protection and/or duplication of signalling. equipment, controls and communications. • Match packages of work and their content to planned periods of track possession. • Highlight options for the separation of general public and work on site.

Group E - Civil engineering
3 - Railways, working adjacent to, maintenance of

E3

Examples of Risk Mitigation (methods of solution)

ACTION \ ISSUE	Facility close to overhead electrification lines	Installation of inspection boxes for maintenance
Avoidance Design to avoid identified hazards but beware of introducing others	Locate facility away from overhead electric lines	Position boxes where access can be obtained away from track side
Reduction Design to reduce identified hazards but beware of increasing others	Design components to require small cranes.	Provide defined and guarded access ways to boxes alongside trackside
Control Design to provide acceptable safeguards for all remaining identified hazards	Outline erection sequences assumed. Place goal posts.	

Examples of Risk Mitigation (issues addressed at different stages)

A distribution warehouse for a mail-order company is to be built on a long rectangular plot of land close to an overhead electrified railway.

Concept design	Scheme design	Detail design
Design the access road to the warehouse to abut the railway land.	The designer favours more and shallower piles rather than fewer deeper piles (taller rigs). The deeper drains will be routed furthest from the railway land.	

A road crosses over a non-electrified railway line. Routine maintenance inspections of the bridge have identified that remedial works are necessary to the parapets of the bridge.

Concept design	Scheme design	Detail design
Consider track status and whether overnight working is necessary. Consult with controllers of track on requirements	Identify methods which do not encroach onto the track, even for track possession periods.	Ensure that the methods of repair have set-up, preparation, and curing periods which are compatible with the times of possession.

GENERAL PLANNING — **A**

EXCAVATIONS AND FOUNDATIONS — **B**

PRIMARY STRUCTURE — **C**

BUILDING ELEMENTS AND BUILDING SERVICES — **D**

CIVIL ENGINEERING — **E3**

A GENERAL PLANNING

B EXCAVATIONS AND FOUNDATIONS

C PRIMARY STRUCTURE

D BUILDING ELEMENTS AND BUILDING SERVICES

E 3 CIVIL ENGINEERING

Related Issues

References within this document

References	Related issues
A2	Site clearance activities will need to consider the local environment.
A4	Access/egress routes will also be determined by local considerations e.g. roads, urban/rural site interface with general public and other transport systems.
A5	Site layout will be determined by working space available and track safety measures required.
B1-B3	Excavation and earthworks will need to consider effects on drainage and permanent way track stability.
C1-C6	Construction materials may require special routes to site and careful consideration with respect to site storage.
D7-D9	Services for power conducting and signalling systems need careful attention.
E1	Working space restrictions especially on small sites accentuate problems.

References for Further Guidance

Primary general references and background information given in Section 4

Primary

- BRB Code GC/TC0014 Requirements for Construction work on or near Railway Land 1994

Secondary

- Railtrack GO/RT3070 Track Safety Handbook 1995
- Esveld, Modern Railway Track
- Railway Group Standards

Background

- Permanent Way Institute, British Railway Track Design, Construction and Maintenance 6th ed. 1995

Classification

CEWS Class A, **CI/SfB** Code (--)11

Read the Introduction (page 9) before using the following guidelines

Scope

- Bridges for and over/under roads, railways, rivers, canals.
  (Includes footbridges, subways, farm bridges, temporary bridges.)
- Bridge strengthening and major repairs.

Exclusions

- Tunnels, piped watercourse, corrugated metal culverts.

Major Hazards

Refer to the Introduction (page 9) for details of accident types and health risks

Falls
Work at height.
Inadequate access.

Intrusions
Collapse of foundation excavation/or cofferdam.
Embankment slip.
Highway traffic.

Services
Overhead and underground cables.
Pipes and cables concealed in the bridge deck.

Buried/crushed/trapped
Collapse of permanent and temporary work during construction.
Trapped under permanent bearing.

Plant and machinery
Struck by plant, or materials and units being slewed into position.
Failure of jack or cables during tensioning.

Health hazards
Concrete additives.
Liquid applied waterproofers.
Hot bitumen.
Contaminated land.

Specific Hazard Identification

Possible key considerations:

- **Stability** - What procedures required for safe erection?
- **Site investigation** - What hazards do ground conditions present?
- **Access/working room** - Where can materials be stored to provide clear/safe access and working space?
- **Services** - Is the site affected by overhead and underground services? Where are the services?
- **The spanned facility** -What particular safety procedures need to be addressed for whatever is crossed?
- **Access** - What facility is required for future maintenance?
- **Public** - What protection methods are required?
- **Any others?**

Prompts

- Site history
- Access routes
- Materials delivery/storage/use
- Contaminated land
- Adjacent structures
- Demolition
- Future maintenance
- Waste disposal

Hazards Consideration in Design

Stage	Considerations and issues	Possible design options to avoid or mitigate hazards identified for bridge construction
Concept Design	• Is a bridge necessary? • Local issues affecting design • Access to site • Overhead/underground services • Ground conditions • Future maintenance.	• Consider reducing the number of piers by increasing the length of spans. • Is the desired profile for wind resistance more safely achieved by shaping the off-site prefabricated structural units or by on-site addition of cladding? • Location of abutment to respect local ground conditions as well as alignment of routes under and over. • Choose structural form and material with respect to future maintenance and appropriateness of prefabrication.
Scheme Design	• Demolition • Sequence of construction • Foundations • Working space • Ground contamination • Hydrology • Services • Materials delivery	• Favour minimum depth of excavation for bridge foundations. • Reduce groundwater problems (that may cause instability) by appropriate drainage measures. • Avoid the need to (temporarily) divert services in advance of construction. • Consider what temporary works are expected and what construction methods are excluded by the nature of the site.
Detail Design	• Storage • Excavation • Temporary structural supports • Lifting measures	• More durable design solutions will reduce the frequency of future maintenance. • Ensure that prefabricated components can be handled practically by choosing symmetrical forms and incorporating lifting points. • Assess whether prefabricated units could incorporate the permanent barriers. • Include facilities for safe access to carry out future inspections and maintenance.

Examples of Risk Mitigation (methods of solution)

ACTION / ISSUE	Vehicle collision with abutment works	Access gantries for maintenance
Avoidance Design to avoid identified hazards but beware of introducing others	Increase span of bridge to obviate need for abutments or allow them further away from road.	Not needed because a permanent means of access is incorporated into the design.
Reduction Design to reduce identified hazards but beware of increasing others	Design a permanent barrier to be installed before abutment work commences and to remain effective throughout construction.	Access routes provided for all internal inspections and all external surfaces are reachable by lorry-mounted equipment.
Control Design to provide acceptable safeguards for all remaining identified hazards	Reduce vehicle speed and/or change routes by traffic control e.g. narrow lanes, closed lanes, contra-flows etc.	Brackets and holes provided at frequent intervals sufficient to construct temporary access to all areas.

Examples of Risk Mitigation (issues addressed at different stages)

An existing road bridge is to be reconstructed. The duration of the works is expected to be twelve months. The location is urban. Local road and pedestrian traffic at peak times is considerable. The bridge crosses a canal.

Concept design	Scheme design	Detail design
What services use the bridge as a crossing? Consider temporary closures and partial closures. Determine usage of canal and tow path.	Co-ordinate the location of a temporary bridge for service diversions, and pedestrian traffic. Bored pile design less likely to disturb canal than driven piles or large excavations.	Consider/provide suitable solution for traffic diversions and public access to properties on each side.

An existing motorway bridge is to be symmetrically widened to accommodate an additional traffic lane on either side.

Concept design	Scheme design	Detail design
Consider construction history and as-built drawings. Assess structure to determine necessary modification or demolition and replace. Additional lane and new hard shoulder? Traffic and access constraints.	Identify methods to reduce worker/road traffic conflict. Consider disruption to road traffic and identify an acceptable sequence of construction.	Identify maintenance and repair strategy for bridge. Review assumed construction methods and sequences.

GENERAL PLANNING **A**

EXCAVATIONS AND FOUNDATIONS **B**

PRIMARY STRUCTURE **C**

BUILDING ELEMENTS AND BUILDING SERVICES **D**

CIVIL ENGINEERING **E 4**

Related Issues

References within this document

References	Related issues
A1	Local environment requires protection from the hazards associated with any construction work.
A2	Site clearance will involve access and demolition problems.
A3	Ground investigations should be comprehensive to allow alternative methods of construction to be investigated.
A4	Access/egress routes may affect the construction method and materials to be used at the site as well as site security and protection of the public.
A5,E1	Site layout working room will determine construction methods and appropriate construction plant to be used.
B1,B3	Excavation/foundation will need to consider drainage and stability problems.
C1-C4	Concrete construction hazards will arise in the foundations, abutments and spanning members.
C5,C6	Structural steelwork construction hazards will arise mainly for the spanning members.
C7	Masonry hazards will arise when facing abutments with stonework or similar.
C8	Timber hazards will arise for small span bridges.
E6	Working over/near water will add additional hazards for bridge construction.

References for Further Guidance

Primary general references and background information given in Section 4

Primary

- HSE GS28 Parts 1 to 4 Safe erection of structures
- CIRIA Report 155 Bridges - design for improved buildability 1996

Secondary

- CIRIA Special Publication 57 Handling of materials on site 1988
- Hardy, Park, Ryall, Bridge management. Inspection, maintenance, assessment and repair

Background

- Thomas Telford, Bridge design for economy and durability
- CIRIA Special Publication 95 The design and construction of sheet-piled cofferdams 1993
- DoT Design Manual for Road and Bridgeworks

Classification

CI/SfB Code (--)182

Read the Introduction (page 9) before using the following guidelines

Scope

- Existing bridges for and over roads, railways, aqueducts, viaducts, footbridges, farm bridges, subways.

  (Maintenance to include: inspection surveys, monitoring, cleaning, and painting.)

Exclusions

- Tunnels, CM culverts, piped watercourses.
- Bridge strengthening and repairs (see E4).

Major Hazards

Refer to the Introduction (page 9) for details of accident types and health risks

Falls
Awkward access.
Unsafe place of work.
Difficult working position.

Plant and machinery
Use of small tools in restricted circumstances.
Struck by access gantries and lifting/slewing operations.

Traffic
Working adjacent road/ railway traffic.
Large vehicles close to work areas under the bridge. Pedestrian routes.

Services
Cables and pipes concealed in the bridge deck.
Electrified rails and overhead cables.

Health hazards
Waterproofing primers.
Paint and solvents. Dust. Skin irritants and allergens.

Asphyxiation
Working in confined spaces. Harmful gases.

A GENERAL PLANNING

B EXCAVATIONS AND FOUNDATIONS

C PRIMARY STRUCTURE

D BUILDING ELEMENTS AND BUILDING SERVICES

E5 CIVIL ENGINEERING

Specific Hazard Identification

Possible key considerations:

- **Bridge location** - What is the bridge type? What does it cross (e.g. water, road or railway?
- **Bridge details** - Clearance, structural form, prestressed elements?
- **Access/working room** - What are suitable plant and equipment for inspection and maintenance?
- **Services** - What services exist within/without structure to be accommodated? Protection/access?
- **Environment** - Will the site or use of the bridge exclude using particular plant or materials?
- **Any others?**

Prompts

- Health and safety file?
- Construction history
- Drawings/manuals
- Ground conditions
- Working platforms
- Confined spaces
- Temporary structures
- Weather conditions
- Services
- Repair materials

Hazards Consideration in Design

Stage	Considerations and issues	Possible design options to avoid or mitigate hazards identified for bridge maintenance
Concept Design		• Review the implications of deferring the maintenance work. • Check demolition and replacement as an alternative to frequent maintenance. • If the extent and scope of work is uncertain, consider further inspections before advancing the design.
Scheme Design	• Bridge type • Access • Environment • Working space • Possessions • Inspection • Ground investigation • Hard standing/platform locations • Fixtures for access assistance • Sequence/phasing • Temporary work • Hazardous materials • Plant and machinery • Services • Task lighting and visibility	• If the work is weather sensitive, define or revise the programme accordingly. • Ensure that the preferred solution takes advantage of new developments in access equipment - e.g. lorry-mounted booms for access to bridge soffits.
Detail Design		• Favour the selection of repair processes with less noise, dust, waste and harmful substances. • Select preparation and application methods which use remotely controlled equipment.

Examples of Risk Mitigation (methods of solution)

ACTION \ ISSUE	Provide temporary access	Hazardous substances
Avoidance Design to avoid identified hazards but beware of introducing others	Use robots, CCTV, and electronic survey methods for remote inspection.	Exclude the use of materials, chemicals and solvents with known risks to health.
Reduction Design to reduce identified hazards but beware of increasing others	Use lorry-mounted access platforms to minimise the time period of men and equipment on site.	Hazardous substances only allowed if they significantly extend the period to first maintenance and reduce frequency of maintenance thereafter.
Control Design to provide acceptable safeguards for all remaining identified hazards	Divert traffic, calm traffic, provide barriers and buffer zones around the erection of traditional scaffolding.	Control of hazardous substances will be managed by principal contractor.

Examples of Risk Mitigation (issues addressed at different stages)

There is serious spalling on the soffit of a concrete bridge deck over a canal.

Concept design	Scheme design	Detail design
Determine whether the work can be effected without compromising the integrity of the bridge. Consider the practicality of using a temporary deck or pontoon for easy access.	Specify lane closures to reduce maximum load on bridge.	Select materials and methods which will allow the works to be broken down into smaller controlled areas.

Waterproofing for a road bridge deck is to minimise water ingress and hence road salt attack in order to reduce maintenance and the hazards associated with working at height.

Concept design	Scheme design	Detail design
Maximise deck cross fall with drainage facility to cater for large rainfall events. Plan bridge closure and/or traffic diversions.	Consider appropriate waterproofing options (sheet materials, liquid coatings, impregnation) and assess their inherent risks to health.	Design for eventual replacement/ ease of repair of waterproofing system.

GENERAL PLANNING — **A**

EXCAVATIONS AND FOUNDATIONS — **B**

PRIMARY STRUCTURE — **C**

BUILDING ELEMENTS AND BUILDING SERVICES — **D**

CIVIL ENGINEERING — **E 5**

E5 Group E - Civil engineering
5 - Bridge maintenance

A GENERAL PLANNING
B EXCAVATIONS AND FOUNDATIONS
C PRIMARY STRUCTURE
D BUILDING ELEMENTS AND BUILDING SERVICES
E 5 CIVIL ENGINEERING

Related Issues

References within this document

References	Related issues
A1	Local environment is affected by maintenance work which invariably disrupts pedestrian and road traffic movements.
A2	Site clearance relates to safe access and storage of materials.
A4	Access/egress to the structure is one of the most important safety aspects of bridge maintenance. Access constraints may also dictate plant/machinery to be used.
A5,E1	Site location/working space will dictate equipment and materials to be used. Confined working accentuates and creates hazards.
B1	Excavation will need to consider effect on drainage and bridge stability.
C1-C6	Construction materials have inherent properties and their method of application may be hazardous to health.
E6	Working over/near water will add hazards to bridge maintenance.

References for Further Guidance

Primary general references and background information given in Section 4

Primary

• Hardy, Park, Ryall, Bridge management. Inspection, maintenance, assessment and repair

Secondary

• HSE GS5 Entry into confined spaces
• CIRIA Report 155 Bridges - design for improved buildability 1996

Background

• Thomas Telford, Bridge design for economy and durability
• DoT Design manual for road and bridgeworks

Classification

CI/SfB Code (--)182 (W2)

Group E - Civil engineering
6 - Working over/near water

Read the Introduction (page 9) before using the following guidelines

Scope

- Inland and coastal waters.

  Including: watercourses, (rivers, canals, ditches), lakes, reservoirs, ponds, tanks, docks, wharves, estuaries, harbours.

Exclusions

- Work in offshore waters.

Major Hazards

Refer to the Introduction (page 9) for details of accident types and health risks

Immersion
Cold water shock.
Hypothermia.
Fatigue.
Drowning.

Moving water
River currents, scour.
Tidal movements.
Flood water.

Services
Electrocution/explosion,
(power cables in water).

Health hazards
Water-borne diseases
(e.g. Weil's Disease).
Contaminated water.
Chemicals.

Crushed/trapped
Impact by boats and pontoons.
Struck by plant or slewed materials
and equipment.

Falls
Slipping on wet surfaces.
Awkward access.
Unstable platforms.

Sidebar tabs:
- GENERAL PLANNING — A
- EXCAVATIONS AND FOUNDATIONS — B
- PRIMARY STRUCTURE — C
- BUILDING ELEMENTS AND BUILDING SERVICES — D
- CIVIL ENGINEERING — E6

A GENERAL PLANNING

B EXCAVATIONS AND FOUNDATIONS

C PRIMARY STRUCTURE

D BUILDING ELEMENTS AND BUILDING SERVICES

E 6 CIVIL ENGINEERING

Specific Hazard Identification

Possible key considerations:

- **Site survey** - What are tidal movements? Any locks, weirs and sluices, etc.?
- **Access/egress** - What is required to make safe with sufficient protection?
- **Working room** - What plant to use? Where to locate plant and materials?
- **Location** - What is the nature of the water (running or still)? Is it sea, river, canal, lake? What is depth and tidal range?
- **Working level** - What are the methods to safeguard falling from height? What emergency procedures are necessary?
- **Any others?**

Prompts

- Guard rails/barriers
- Protection of public
- Contamination
- Illumination
- Weather conditions
- Seasonal changes

Hazards Consideration in Design

Stage	Considerations and issues	Possible design options to avoid or mitigate hazards identified for working over/near water
Concept Design		• Choose a prefabricated construction to avoid/minimise fabrication over water. • Divert or exclude the water by dams and pumping. • Consider temporary infilling or a grillage of pontoons to exclude or isolate the water. • Check whether working space or bed conditions exclude any construction methods.
Scheme Design	• Site survey • Water type/depth • Location • Services • Geotechnical investigation • Working space • Contamination • Safe access • Advance works (services, drainage) • Excavations • Emergency procedures • Sequence of operations	• Ascertain a programme and design for the works to be carried out at low tide only. • Maximise the types of component which could be prefabricated. • Examine sequences of working to minimise period of exposure.
Detail Design		• Select more durable materials and finishes for surfaces which require maintenance access over water (i.e. fewer visits required). • New works to include provision for future maintenance access where possible.

Examples of Risk Mitigation (methods of solution)

ISSUE / ACTION	Excavation in marshland
Avoidance Design to avoid identified hazards but beware of introducing others	No excavation would be required for a structure designed to be fabricated off-site and then ballasted to "float" at the required level.
Reduction Design to reduce identified hazards but beware of increasing others	The use of prefabricated tanks as the base units for all the large structures of the development would reduce excavation to the link buildings/corridors.
Control Design to provide acceptable safeguards for all remaining identified hazards	Design a cofferdam for the excavation of material from within. The internal water level would be controlled by pumping and the cofferdam could be incorporated into the permanent works.

Examples of Risk Mitigation (issues addressed at different stages)

A small road bridge is required across a shallow but navigable canal used by narrow boats. A lock is immediately downstream. The towpath is in constant use.

Concept design	Scheme design	Detail design
Review the options for a pre-fabricated/pre-cast bridge or components to minimise the work on site.	Match the size and weight of precast components to a practicable size and location of mobile crane.	Design piles which can be installed by piling plant without intruding into the towpath and footway access. Allow space for safe delivery and stockpile of materials.

A new suspension bridge is to cross a wide river. The steel prefabricated hollow section deck is to carry a 6 lane highway. Water clearance is 30m. A suitable road lighting system is to be provided.

Concept design	Scheme design	Detail design
Appropriate illumination could be provided from edge of deck or centrally. Coordinate spacing of lights with cables and hangers and consider access for future maintenance.	Consider "drop down" columns for easier maintenance, and a permanent barrier protected corridor which accesses every lamp post.	Make the whole lamp post, lamp unit, and wiring by off-site fabrication, so that only deck level connections are necessary on site.

A — GENERAL PLANNING

B — EXCAVATIONS AND FOUNDATIONS

C — PRIMARY STRUCTURE

D — BUILDING ELEMENTS AND BUILDING SERVICES

E 6 — CIVIL ENGINEERING

Related Issues

References within this document

References	Related issues
A4	Ground investigation will identify ground water levels and water quality.
A3	Access/egress routes for materials delivery and waste disposal will be determined by local conditions.
A5	Site layout will be determined by project under construction in relation to space available (water authority may have specific site rules).
B1-B7	Excavation, drainage effects and support solutions could be crucial. Dewatering/exclusion of water will be important considerations.
C1-C8	Construction components and materials may require special routes within the site and storage may also be a problem.
D8	Electrical services mean electrocution is a major hazard when working near water.

References for Further Guidance

Primary general references and background information given in Section 4

Primary

- Construction Industry Training Board (CITB), Construction site safety notes No.30 GE 700//30 Working over water 1992
- Building Employers Confederation (BEC), Construction safety, Section 8E Working over water 1988
- CIRIA Special Publication 130 Site safety for the water industry 1997

Secondary

- CIRIA Special Publication 57 Handling of materials on site 1988

Background

- BS 8093: 1991 Code of practice for the use of safety nets containment nets and sheets on constructional works

Classification

CI/SfB   Code (--)13

Read the Introduction (page 9) before using the following guidelines

Scope

- Cofferdams (in water, near water, in saturated ground).

Exclusions

- Cofferdams in off-shore environments (generally subject to extensive wave pressures and aggressive climate).
- Pressurised working.

Major Hazards

Refer to the Introduction (page 9) for details of accident types and health risks

Crushed/trapped
Collisions between boats, pontoons, crane barges, and cofferdam. Moving plant and slewed equipment in confined space.

Falls
From dam wall into excavation or into water.

Inundation
Failure of cofferdam walls (due to water pressure/scour/impact). Base failure (piping/heave).

Water
Cold water shock.
Tidal movements.
Currents and scour.
Drowning.

Health hazards
Contaminated ground water. Weil's Disease. Noxious gases in confined spaces. Noise and vibration from piling.

Services
Cables in river-bed. Temporary power cables in water. Fuel lines and storage.

A GENERAL PLANNING

B EXCAVATIONS AND FOUNDATIONS

C PRIMARY STRUCTURE

D BUILDING ELEMENTS AND BUILDING SERVICES

E 7 CIVIL ENGINEERING

Specific Hazard Identification

Possible key considerations:

- **Project** - Can the cofferdam be wholly incorporated into the permanent structure?
- **Site investigation** - What is water table variation and extent of ground contamination? What is the underwater topography? Are there any obstructions?
- **Access** - What constraints affect movement of personnel, plant and machinery and materials delivery?
- **Adjacent water** - Is water running/still, navigable, liable to level variation, tidal, marine?
- **Environment** -What adjacent features/structures may be affected?
- **Working height** - Minimised by prefabrication of cofferdam?
- **Removal** - Will the permanent works obstruct the removal of temporary cofferdams?
- **Any others?**

Prompts

- Project programmes
- Ground conditions
- Water levels/depths
- Contaminants/health
- Illumination
- Weather conditions
- Emergency escape routes
- Safe access
- Services
- Removal/reinstatement
- Maintenance

Hazards Consideration in Design

Stage	Considerations and issues	Possible design options to avoid or mitigate hazards identified for cofferdams
Concept Design		• Impact by water traffic and floating debris may be resisted by the cofferdam or separate outer defences. • Consider the wider value of a temporary causeway instead of floating rigs. • Prefabricated caissons towed into place are quieter and involve less work in the water than driven piled cofferdams.
Scheme Design	• Why the cofferdam? • Underwater survey • Adjacent water feature • Access • Environment • Ground investigation • Contamination • Programme of works • Working height • Support system • Stability • Services • Noise	• Check the working platform/causeway level with respect to high tide/flood records and the intended season of works. • Provide scope for structural enhancement to respond to adverse monitoring reports. • Design plan shape of cofferdam to suit working space and construction plant as well as final structure.
Detail Design		• Design out the need for underwater working by using a different construction or remotely controlled techniques . • Design in features for safe access, (e.g. holes and lugs for quick and easy fixing of equipment). • Coordinate the design of in-situ walings with permanent structure to minimise the extent of breaking out.

Examples of Risk Mitigation (methods of solution)

ACTION	ISSUE: Floating cranage and piling plant
Avoidance Design to avoid identified hazards but beware of introducing others	The use of heavy floating plant could be avoided by building the cofferdam off-site on land or in a dry dock. Instead, tug-boats would manoeuvre the floating cofferdam into position for sinking into place.
Reduction Design to reduce identified hazards but beware of increasing others	For a multi-span bridge over water, the sites of foundations in shallower waters could be accessed by building a temporary causeway for land-based plant to construct the cofferdams.
Control Design to provide acceptable safeguards for all remaining identified hazards	The project planning and contract periods are based on the assumption that the use of floating plant is only practicable at the turn of the tide and in good weather.

Examples of Risk Mitigation (issues addressed at different stages)

A large cofferdam is required for a bridge foundation in a river.

Concept design	Scheme design	Detail design
Consider permanent structure to be constructed. Consider effects on local marine movements to determine working space available.	Assume space available for double skin earth filled parallel walls. Provides safer working area, no internal strutting.	Wall design, drainage design, need for cross walls, include flexible and convenient details for the addition of working platforms.

A warehouse with deep basement storage is to be constructed adjacent to a navigable river - excavation for the foundation of the building is in saturated alluvial material.

Concept design	Scheme design	Detail design
Consider adjacent structures and environment to determine appropriate cofferdam type. Assume an external support.	Multi-level ground anchors or raking piles (instead of walings) provide safer working areas by being less intrusive into the confined space.	Consider the stability of adjacent structures and river bank, and review options for ground works in the intervening space to minimise their risk exposure. Include ground water and earth pressure monitoring devices to guide future maintenance/remedial work.

GENERAL PLANNING — A

EXCAVATIONS AND FOUNDATIONS — B

PRIMARY STRUCTURE — C

BUILDING ELEMENTS AND BUILDING SERVICES — D

CIVIL ENGINEERING — E7

A
GENERAL PLANNING

B
EXCAVATIONS
AND FOUNDATIONS

C
PRIMARY STRUCTURE

D
BUILDING ELEMENTS
AND BUILDING SERVICES

E
7
CIVIL ENGINEERING

Related Issues

References within this document

References	Related issues
A1,B6	Local environment is affected by piling which gives rise to noise and vibration. The effects on local buildings, industry and the general public must be considered.
A3	Access/egress routes for materials delivery and waste removal may also be dictated by local environment.
A4	Ground investigation is an important consideration in choice of support system.
B1,B2	Excavations inside cofferdams mean crucial considerations include ground conditions, drainage effects, support solutions and dewatering.
C1-C8	Foundations and Primary Structure may be constructed inside cofferdams.
D8	Electrical services mean electrocution is a major hazard when working near water.
E6	Working near water will involve additional hazards.

References for Further Guidance

Primary general references and background information given in Section 4

Primary

- CIRIA Special Publication 95 The design and construction of sheet piled cofferdams 1993

Secondary

- CIRIA Special Publication 57 Handling of materials on site 1988
- Tomlinson, Foundation design and construction
- British Steel Corporation (BSC) Piling Handbook

Background

Classification

CI/SfB Code (--)187

Group E - Civil engineering
8 - Pipes and cables

E8

Read the Introduction (page 9) before using the following guidelines

Scope

- Pipes: carrying water, sewage, gas, oil, etc. or used as protection for cables and "piped" services.
- Cables: for power, telephone, TV, other communications cables.

Exclusions

- Power cables for railways.
- Trenches (see B3).

Major Hazards

Refer to the Introduction (page 9) for details of accident types and health risks

Falls
From construction and maintenance plant and equipment.
Into trenches and excavations. From suspended cable locations.

Buried/crushed/trapped
Struck by plant and machinery.
Collapse of trench or excavation.

Services
Overhead and underground power cables.
Gas and fuel pipelines.
Sewers.
Emergency communications.

Health hazards
Contaminated ground and water (e.g. Weil's Disease).
Sewage and other effluents.
Noise.
Dust.

Asphyxiation
Working in confined spaces and access chambers.
Harmful gases.

Traffic
Cabling over roads/ railways.
Runaway vehicles entering area of work.
Access chambers in the highway.

A GENERAL PLANNING

B EXCAVATIONS AND FOUNDATIONS

C PRIMARY STRUCTURE

D BUILDING ELEMENTS AND BUILDING SERVICES

E8 CIVIL ENGINEERING

A — GENERAL PLANNING

B — EXCAVATIONS AND FOUNDATIONS

C — PRIMARY STRUCTURE

D — BUILDING ELEMENTS AND BUILDING SERVICES

E8 — CIVIL ENGINEERING

Specific Hazard Identification

Possible key considerations:

- **Facility** - What type of pipe or wire? What is it conveying?
- **Site survey** - What are site conditions? What other services are present (overhead or underground)? How high, how deep are they? What ground contaminants are present?
- **Working room** - Is there sufficient space for plant and machinery?
- **Environment** - Is work next to structures, buildings, road, railway, also near to water? Special procedures?
- **Access:** What site access route problems exist?
- **Interface** - With utilities and services to buildings/structures.
- **Any others?**

Prompts

- Ground conditions
- What service?
- Contamination
- Access
- Possession
- Maintenance
- Confined spaces (access chambers)

Hazards Consideration in Design

Stage	Considerations and issues	Possible design options to avoid or mitigate hazards identified for pipes and cables
Concept Design		• Review current data to determine the benefit of tracing or surveying some of the existing services. • Review the possibility of co-ordinating the work with planned work by other utilities to streamline construction operations and reduce public disruption.
Scheme Design	• Site location • Access • Possession • Type of pipe/cable • Height and depth • Services • Ground conditions • Adjacent features • Sequence • Working space • Maintenance • Local environment (type of conduit/ temperature control) • Other services	• Plan the route to avoid existing services and minimise the likelihood of disturbance by other construction activity. • Ensure that the design provides for easy location and access to make future connections.
Detail Design		• Whenever possible choose details which anticipate technical change. • Balance the provision of convenient, safe access for future maintenance against easy access by untrained or unauthorised persons.

Group E - Civil engineering
8 - Pipes and cables

E8 box on right

E8

Examples of Risk Mitigation (methods of solution)

ACTION \ ISSUE	In-trench jointing of pipes	Crossing a major road
Avoidance Design to avoid identified hazards but beware of introducing others	Select a pipe/duct capable of being laid from a "reel" located above ground.	Route the service over an existing bridge or micro-bore under the road.
Reduction Design to reduce identified hazards but beware of increasing others	Choose quick and simple jointing (e.g. push-fit or hinged clamps instead of lead filled or welded connections).	Connect excavations on each side of the carriageway by pipe-jacking a service duct between them.
Control Design to provide acceptable safeguards for all remaining identified hazards	Locate complicated joints where wider excavation is possible and likely.	Design for construction in short lengths to suit an acceptable sequence of lane closures.

Examples of Risk Mitigation (issues addressed at different stages)

A new sewer is to be laid in an urban environment. Records have identified underground power cables which cross the alignment and sometimes run parallel to the alignment.

Concept design	Scheme design	Detail design
Re-examine route of sewer to avoid underground services.	Prove information by trial pits and electro-magnetic tracing. Determine the width of working corridor required. Consider use of trenchless techniques. Route cannot be changed.	Trenchless techniques chosen. Specify location of access pits and alignment of sewer to avoid existing services.

To release development land an underground network of pipes for power station cooling water has to be partially replaced and diverted.

Concept design	Scheme design	Detail design
Consider the future maintenance benefit of a whole new network. Review alternative routes and combinations of overhead and underground alignments.	Favour options which allow complete construction of the new routes before breaking into the existing network.	Maintain access to live services during construction. Define the working zone to minimise overlap between construction activities and the operation of the power station.

GENERAL PLANNING — A

EXCAVATIONS AND FOUNDATIONS — B

PRIMARY STRUCTURE — C

BUILDING ELEMENTS AND BUILDING SERVICES — D

CIVIL ENGINEERING — E8

CDM Regulations - work sector guidance for designers   167   CIRIA Report 166   (E8-3)

Related Issues

References within this document

References	Related issues
A1	Surrounding environment will be affected by pipe and cable work (including maintenance operations).
A2	Demolition of a structure must include identification and marking of services that are isolated or redundant. The Health and safety file should be available.
A4	Access/egress routes and facilities for maintenance should be free from obstruction.
B3	Trench excavations must be suitably supported.
E2	Working space for pipes and cables are invariably adjacent to or under roadways. When traffic measures are required during construction or maintenance, consider space and barriers to protect site personnel.

References for Further Guidance

Primary general references and background information given in Section 4

Primary

- HSE HS(G)47 Avoiding danger from underground services
- HSE GS6 Avoidance of danger from overhead electric lines
- HSE CIS 8 (revised) Safety in excavations
- CIRIA Special Publication 57 Handling of materials on site 1988

Secondary

- CIRIA Report 97 Trenching practice 1992
- CIRIA Technical Note 127 Trenchless construction for underground services 1987
- CIRIA Funders Report CP/12 Trenchless and minimum excavation technology: Planning and investigation

Background

- DoT Chapter 8 Traffic Signs Manual
- HSE IND (G) 84L - Leptospirosis: are you at risk?

Classification

CI/SfB   Code (--)I/J

3 Documenting design decisions on individual projects

3.1 THE PROVISION AND USE OF HEALTH AND SAFETY INFORMATION

Designers have a duty to provide information on the significant risks in the design which cannot be avoided. This is provided to other parties involved in the project.

In addition, designers may also wish to document the health and safety considerations made during the design, to keep track of hazards that have not yet been resolved or to indicate the range of design options that were considered at any stage. This need not create a significant burden of extra paperwork. Many organisations already use management systems such as Quality Assurance, and undertake design reviews. Recording the consideration of health and safety in the design will form one part of any such system.

3.2 STATUTORY INFORMATION FOR REGULATION 13(2)(b)

Regulation 13(2)(b) requires designers to produce information as part of their design, which may then be placed in the health and safety plan and/or the health and safety file. In order that the quantity of information to be provided does not grow out of proportion, there are limits as follows:

- designers are not required to provide information on hazards or risks which have been eliminated from the design
- designers only have to provide information on hazards or risks to the extent necessary to enable a competent contractor to properly identify and assess the risks and put appropriate precautions in place.

The effect of the first limit is to concentrate on the residual hazards and risks, i.e. those that the designer has been unable to eliminate and cannot reasonably reduce any further. The second limit means that designers do not have to warn contractors about the hazards and risks which a competent contractor would be able to identify and deal with. Taken together, these limits should go a long way to focussing on significant hazard and risk information.

3.3 INFORMATION FOR IN-HOUSE RECORDS

Designers may like to keep their own records of the hazards they have identified and how they have dealt with the associated risks. These will be discussed during design reviews and progress meetings and the appropriate records could form part of the existing systems for project management. There will be practical reasons to keep records, in case of personnel changes, unexpected delays in the progress of the design, or in case of future dispute.

This guidance does not prescribe how designers should record their considerations and decisions arising from compliance with the CDM Regulation, as each practice will have its own approach when establishing procedures and audit trails. Some guidance on how in-house information might be recorded can be found in CIRIA Report 145 *CDM Regulations - case study guidance for designers: An interim report*. This report was published when the Regulations came into force and therefore does not incorporate any practical experience of implementing the Regulations.

Designers may find it helpful to develop standard forms for recording the health and safety decisions for their projects. This may include the actions they have been able to take to avoid, reduce or provide control measures for the hazards and risks. Such forms may also include a consideration by the designer of whether the residual risk is sufficiently significant or unusual to be outside the scope of a competent contractor in the context of the project, and therefore a candidate for inclusion in the health and safety plan or file.

4 Primary general references and background information

The references given below and in each of the work sectors in Section 2 were correct at the date of publication. However, reference documents are liable to be updated, superseded or withdrawn and readers are urged to check that they have obtained the most up-to-date references.

1. **HEALTH AND SAFETY COMMISSION**
   Managing Construction for health and safety
   Construction (Design and Management) Regulations 1994
   Approved Code of Practice L54
   HSE Books 1995 ISBN 0 7176 0792 5

2. **HEALTH AND SAFETY COMMISSION**
   A guide to managing health and safety in construction
   HSE Books 1995 ISBN 0 7176 0755 0

3. **HEALTH AND SAFETY COMMISSION**
   Designing for health and safety in construction
   HSE Books 1995 ISBN 0 7176 0807 7

4. **HEALTH AND SAFETY EXECUTIVE**
   Health and safety in construction HS(G)150
   HSE Books 1996 ISBN 0 7176 0806 9

5. **HEALTH AND SAFETY EXECUTIVE ***
   Protecting the public - your next move HS(G)151
   HSE Books 1997 ISBN 0 7176 1148 5

6. **HEALTH AND SAFETY EXECUTIVE**
   Information on site safety for designers of smaller building projects
   Bone S. Contract Research Report 72
   HSE Books 1995 ISBN 0 7176 0777 1

7. **HEALTH AND SAFETY EXECUTIVE**
   Dust and noise in the construction process
   Ferguson I. Contract Research Report 73
   HSE Books 1995 ISBN 0 7176 0768 2

8. **HEALTH AND SAFETY EXECUTIVE**
   Seven steps to successful substitution of hazardous substances HS(G)110
   HSE Books 1994 ISBN 0 7176 0695 3

9. **THE BUILDERS EMPLOYERS CONFEDERATION AND BUILDING ADVISORY SERVICE**
   Construction Safety
   Construction Industry Publications Ltd ISBN 1 85263 0027 (frequently updated)

10. **CONSTRUCTION INDUSTRY TRAINING BOARD (CITB)**
    Construction Site Safety
    Safety Notes GE700 (frequently updated). Fourth (Revised) Edition 1992
    Published by CITB ISBN 1 85751 010 0

11. **BIELBY, SC**
    Site safety: A handbook for young construction professionals (2nd edition)
    CIRIA Special Publication 130, 1997 ISBN 0 86017 455 710.

12. **DAVIES, V.J AND TOMASIN, K**
    Construction safety handbook, chap 4 - Hazards of construction and their prevention.
    Thomas Telford 1990 ISBN 0 7277 1385 X

13. **KING, R.W AND HUDSON, R**
    Construction hazard and safety handbook
    Butterworth 1985 ISBN 0 4080 1347 8

14. **WALLER, R.A**
    Planning to reduce noise exposure in construction
    CIRIA Technical Note 138, 1990 ISBN 0 8601 7317 8

    * To be published in summer 1997